Morgann's Essay on the Dramatic Character of Sir John Falstaff

MORGANN'S
ESSAY ON THE
DRAMATIC CHARACTER
OF
SIR JOHN FALSTAFF

EDITED BY

WILLIAM ARTHUR GILL

LONDON
HENRY FROWDE
1912

OXFORD : HORACE HART
PRINTER TO THE UNIVERSITY

INTRODUCTION

MAURICE MORGANN was a man of some influence in politics and literature, though of too
retiring a disposition to catch the eye of the
general public. As an author he was always
anonymous, and sometimes his reserve went
further, as for instance when he refused a pressing
demand for a second edition of the Falstaff
essay, or when he strictly enjoined his executrix
to destroy compositions of his which, according
to an intelligent critic, 'would have planted
a permanent laurel on his grave.' In politics
again he seems to have preferred exercising his
great abilities in other men's names to coming
forward as his own spokesman. Such a nature
is not likely to make much impression on
contemporary records, and several important
questions about Morgann's life are still un-
answered.

Morgann was born in London in 1726 and
died there in 1802. He is said to have come of
'an antient and respectable family in Wales',
but beyond this we know nothing of his parent-

A 2

INTRODUCTION

age ; and the events of his youth and of the
earlier part of his manhood are left to conjecture.
At the age of thirty-five he emerges in the
official lists of the 'Court and City Kalendar'
as 'Weigher and Teller' at the Mint with
a yearly salary 'for himself and clerk' of
£142 10s.,—a position which he retained to
the end of his life. A colleague of his at the
Mint for many years was George Selwyn, as
'Surveyor of the Meltings and Clerk of the
Irons', with a salary 'for himself and clerk'
of £132 10s., and Selwyn's successor was the
Hon. Spencer Perceval. The appointment to
this sinecure proves that Morgann had influence
of some sort, but throws little light on his occupa-
tions. In 1766, when he was forty, he became
an Under-Secretary of State. He had somehow
gained—how he had gained it is one of the un-
answered questions—an uncommonly thorough
knowledge of American affairs, and he was
appointed 'Secretary of the American Depart-
ment' under Lord Shelburne, then for the first
time, at the age of twenty-nine, Secretary of State.
In this office, and in troubled times, Morgann
showed himself clear-sighted and liberal as well
as accurately informed, and we know from memo-
randa of his addressed to his young chief and from
the latter's course meanwhile that his views re-

ceived as much notice in the Government councils as Lord Shelburne was able to obtain for them. A friend of Morgann's has asserted that if 'his sollicitous and enlightened representations had experienced attention, the temporary and the abiding evils of the American contest would not have existed'. There is no doubt at least that his representations were enlightened.

After this he was sent by Lord Shelburne, we are told, 'across the Atlantic as the intended legislator of Canada.' This must have been in 1767 or 1768, for he gave up the Under-secretary-ship in the former year, and Lord Shelburne's official connexion with the colonies ceased in the latter, and was not renewed until 1782, at which time Morgann was otherwise engaged. It is probable that he retired from his Government office in 1767 in order to undertake the Canadian mission, the nature and course of which can only be inferred. General Carleton, who was then acting as Governor-General, is known to have opposed a scheme put forward by Lord Shelburne about 1766 for providing Canada with a Council and Assembly. While this and other points of local administration remained unsettled,—it was even disputed under which laws the Canadians were living, French or British,—there was matter enough for an envoy of the Home Government to examine on the spot. If it is implied in the words, 'the intended legislator of Canada,' that Morgann's powers went beyond examining and reporting, the exercise of them was doubtless conditional, and there is no reason to think that he actually did more than collect information and confer with Carleton. In 1769 Carleton crossed to London to answer questions and advocate his own ideas, and it is probable that Morgann — Lord Shelburne having already withdrawn from office—returned at least as soon. He and Carleton had become good friends, and during the next four years they must often have met in London, and considering Morgann's liberal views and his recent local studies we may assume with some reason that he was no stranger to the framing of the Quebec Act of 1774,—in which Carleton certainly had a large part,—and that he thus helped to obtain for French Canada the corner-stone of her political and religious liberty.

The next time we find Morgann with a special employment is in 1782, or a dozen years after his Canadian mission, and this long blank interval may serve to raise the question whether he had any regular profession or not. He has been described as a 'clerk in the Foreign Office', and it would agree well enough with most of his recorded doings to assume that he was normally a Government official. There are difficulties in the way, however. Apart from the fact that the Foreign Office did not come into existence till Morgann was nearly sixty, it does not appear from the extant lists of officials that Morgann belonged to any Government office during most of his life, if we except his more or less nominal connexion with the Mint. He may have given private help to Lord Shelburne and perhaps to other statesmen oftener than we know, but such occupation can only have been intermittent, and on the whole the conjecture that his ordinary position was that of a gentleman of leisure, with some small inherited income, who occasionally served the State, —though never as a member of Parliament,— seems permissible.

Anyway, we do not hear of him doing anything but literary work of an unlucrative kind between 1770 and 1782. In the latter year he crossed the Atlantic again, going to New York as official Secretary to Carleton, who had just been appointed Commander-in-chief. They sailed from England in March, and by the end of April Morgann was busy at head-quarters in Manhattan, where his sagacity and knowledge found an opening suited to them. Fighting was less needed than statesmanship at this stage of the Revolutionary War; indeed, Carleton went out with the double title, 'Commander-in-chief and Commissioner for restoring peace.' A treaty was being spoken of; the prospect required the British in America to show as much conciliation as prudence and dignity permitted; moreover, the Government at home, in order to shape its proposals to the best advantage, needed an accurate running comment upon the changes in American feeling and other conditions as they occurred. The usefulness of Morgann in these circumstances proved to be such that, about the middle of his stay in New York, he was specially rewarded, at the King's request, with a life-pension of £250 a year and a considerable grant of ready money. He returned home in July, 1783, after an absence of fifteen months, to give Lord North, then Prime Minister, a verbal report and the benefit of his experience in the last stage of the negotiations. When the treaty of peace was signed, he was appointed Secretary of the Embassy charged with the ratification of it,—in acknowledgement, no doubt, of his share in the result,—and in 1784 he received a second official sinecure, worth £200 a year, as one of the four Commissioners of the Hackney Coach Office. At this point his active career, so far as we know, came to an end, though he lived on for another eighteen years. He settled at Knightsbridge, where he owned a house, and it was there that he died.

Of Morgann's personality two good sketches have been preserved in out-of-the-way places— the one in a footnote to a 'Life of Milton' published two years after his death, the other in the preface to an obscure poem on 'The Pleasures of Conversation', which appeared in 1807. The 'Life of Milton' was by a literary clergyman, Dr. Charles Symmons, son of John Symmons, a Welsh squire, who represented Cardiganshire in Parliament from 1746 to 1761. Morgann was intimate with three generations of the Symmons family. As a young man he frequented the town house of John Symmons, and Charles (some thirty years his junior) speaks of him as one 'who has fondled my infancy in his arms, who was the friend of my youth, who expanded the liberality of my opening heart and first taught me to think and to judge'. Morgann, who seems to have been a lifelong bachelor, became as devoted to Charles's children as he had been to their father, and to one of them, John, we indirectly owe some information about his doings in America, for this young man handed over to the safe keeping of the Royal Institution a collection of official papers which Morgann had brought back from New York and given to him. John was a barrister, and another barrister—a friend of his—called William Cooke, seems to have lived with Morgann in his latter years, possibly as his secretary. Cooke was the author of the poem on the ' Pleasures of Conversation '.

Morgann appears in these sketches as an urbane old gentleman, used to fashionable society and to intercourse with 'the great', 'highly placed', but simple and disinterested,—(' small as his disinterestedness had suffered his fortune to remain ',)—one who ' from a long intercourse with the world acquired no suspicion or hardness, but with the simplicity and candour retained to the last the cheerfulness and sensibility of childhood '. His rectitude, his benevolence, his hatred of cruelty and oppression are insisted upon, but he stands out most clearly perhaps as a spirited *causeur*, ' the charm of every society he mixed with,' displaying ' the happiest arts of badinage and pleasantry ', who ' even when he was in error continued to be specious and to please, and never failed of your applause, though he might sometimes of your assent '. His ' creative fancy ', it seems, ' branched upon such an infinite variety of views as made it sometimes

difficult for him to settle upon the close point,
but when he gained that point (which he generally did) with what eloquence and perspicuity
did he support it ! With what energies did the
heart speak ! Nay, even when he missed it, he
led us through such a delightful labyrinth of
fragrance and flowers as induced us to forget the
disappointment.'

'His leisure hours', Cooke tells us, 'were
frequently employed upon some curious or in-
teresting literary subject,' and Charles Symmons,
mentioning the destruction of papers after his
death, deplores particularly the loss of 'some in
the walks of politics, metaphysics and criticism'.
It is possible that some of his publications are
still unidentified, since he wrote anonymously.
Those identified are the Falstaff essay, and
pamphlets on a national militia, the slave trade,
the prevention of adultery, and the state of France
in 1794. Boswell, who calls the Falstaff essay
' very ingenious ', records two particular meetings
between Morgann and Dr. Johnson. On the one
occasion the pair had a dispute ' pretty late at
night ', and Johnson ' would not give up though
he was in the wrong ', but he acknowledged his
error next morning at breakfast ; on the other,
Morgann broke down the doctor's pretended
admiration of a poetaster by provoking him diplo-

matically to the celebrated admission, 'Sir, there is no settling the point of precedency between a louse and a flea.'

The *Essay on the Dramatic Character of Sir John Falstaff* was written in 1774, laid aside for some time, and revised and published in 1777, when Morgann was fifty-one and, as he says, ' unengaged'. A second edition was soon called for, but, being withheld at his wish during his lifetime, did not appear till 1820. In 1825 a publisher saw reason to bring the essay out a third time ; and the present is the fourth edition.

Morgann speaks of his work as 'a mere experiment . . . attended by all the difficulties and dangers of Novelty'. He might claim novelty for it upon two grounds. No previous study of a single character of Shakespeare's had been carried out on so elaborate a scale, and it seems that by the mere size of his example Morgann stimulated a branch of Shakespearian criticism that was soon to flourish greatly. Secondly,—and here he has had fewer imitators, —he regarded his subject from a new point of view.

Writers about Shakespeare's characters appear usually to be prompted by one or more of

the following motives : to inquire into human
nature itself, the persons in the plays being taken
simply as real persons, like those in history ; to inquire into Shakespeare's conception and estimate
of human nature ; to discover how the dramatist
adapts human nature to the forms of his art.
Morgann contends—and this is his special point
of view—that the third of these enterprises should
come first,—that we must begin by ascertaining
how far the character is modified by the dramatic
medium in which it is presented, before we can
hope to learn anything certain from it either about
human nature or about Shakespeare's conception
and estimate of human nature.

The title of the essay carefully indicates this
contention when it sets forth the subject as, not
simply 'the character', but 'the dramatic character' of Falstaff,—that is, an adjusted character,
arranged and manipulated by the craftsman for
a particular occasion, with some features deliber-
ately blurred or diminished and others deliber-
ately thrown forward ; a character in an 'artificial
condition' ; in short, a 'theatric form',—these
two expressions, 'artificial condition' and
'theatric form', being used by Morgann as
synonymous with 'dramatic character'. He
argues in effect : if we did not instinctively,
before a picture of a group of people, allow for

some influences of the artist's general scheme, of the contrasting juxtaposition of figures, and so on, what strange assertions we might make about the colouring and anatomy of the originals; and what kind of information about human nature, or about Shakespeare's conception of it, are we likely to obtain from the 'theatric form' of Falstaff, if the peculiarities or refractions of his presentation in the play are not distinguished and discounted first?

Morgann analysed his subject from this point of view with all the qualities of a great critic, except one : the essay is poorly arranged. The truth is, it overflowed its plan in the course of writing. Setting out for a piece of scholarly diversion, for a critical *jeu d'esprit*,—the defence of Falstaff from the charge of cowardice,—Morgann was soon tempted into a more serious inquiry and went deeper in it than his original plan allowed. He was reluctant to go so far, it seems, or at least was fully aware of something amorphous in the consequences. He deplores his lapses from the intended airy strain, and says in his preface : 'If the book shall be fortunate enough to obtain another impression, a separation may be made, and such of the heavier parts as cannot be wholly dispensed with sink to their proper station—a Note.' When a second impression was called for, he probably did not refuse the demand until he had convinced himself that he could not harmonize his work by removing the heavier parts to the margin without destroying it.   The observant reader, however, who is prepared for some confusion, will probably find clues enough scattered about to save him from being often at a loss.

The essay is both a study of Falstaff and a study of Shakespeare, and the value of its point of view may be put to a double test. We may first compare it with other appreciations of the Knight which have a different point of view,—with Johnson's or Hazlitt's, for instance.   These accounts are so much shorter than Morgann's that the sense of familiarity which comes from abundance of detail cannot be expected of them in the same measure ; but the reader who turns from them to our essay may feel in it, apart from this, a deeper kind of intimacy which is due to its method.   Morgann, he will perhaps feel, has a passport which enables him to go behind the scenes and to speak with the accent of certainty, where Johnson and Hazlitt, through their indifference to the 'artificial condition', are comparatively superficial and unconvincing. They seem to be fumbling at a lock with keys which do not quite fit it. Morgann received some suggestions, no doubt, from Johnson's remarks on Falstaff, and the similarity of ideas, so far as it goes, makes the distinction of method all the plainer.

And then our author's guiding conception has enabled him to make a singularly penetrating exploration of the mind of the craftsman of the 'theatric form'. 'Falstaff is the word, but Shakespeare is the theme,' says Morgann, about his essay, and the reader will agree with him. He does not concern himself much with Shakespeare as a man, a poet, or a philosopher, but he flashes on us some glimpses so far-reaching into the *technique* and creative efforts of the dramatist that a reverent spectator might almost feel a little hesitation in taking advantage of them, as if he were trespassing on sacred mysteries.

NOTE

A few obvious misprints, in addition to those noticed in the *Errata* (p. 186) of the edition of 1777, have been corrected. But many harmless irregularities have been left unaltered in the reprint, which follows its original by page and line. And some doubtful readings have been given the benefit of the doubt.

AN

E   S   S   A   Y

ON

SHAKESPEARE's *FALSTAFF*.

A N

E S S A Y

ON THE

DRAMATIC CHARACTER

OF

Sir *J O H N   F A L S T A F F*.

I am not *John of Gaunt* your Grandfather, but yet
no COWARD, *Hal*.

Firſt Part of HENRY IV.

L O N D O N:

PRINTED FOR T. D A V I E S, IN RUSSEL-STREET,
COVENT GARDEN.

MDCCLXXVII.

PREFACE.

THE following sheets were written in consequence of a friendly conversation, turning by some chance upon the Character of FALSTAFF, wherein the Writer, maintaining contrary to the general Opinion, that, this Character was not intended to be shewn as a Coward, he was challenged to deliver and support that Opinion from the Press, with an engagement, now he fears forgotten, for it was three years ago, that he should be answered thro' the

A   same

fame channel : Thus ftimulated, thefe papers were almoft wholly written in a very fhort time, but not without thofe attentions, whether fuccefsful or not, which feemed neceffary to carry them beyond the Prefs into the hands of the Public. From the influence of the foregoing circumftances it is, that the Writer has generally affumed rather the character and tone of an Advocate than of an Inquirer ;—though if he had not firft *inquired* and been *convinced,* he fhould never have attempted to

have

have amufed either himfelf or others with the fubject.—The impulfe of the occafion, however, being paffed, the papers were thrown by, and almoft forgotten: But having been looked into of late by fome friends, who obferving that the Writer had not enlarged fo far for the fake of FALSTAFF alone, but that the Argument was made fubfervient to Critical amufement, perfuaded him to revife and convey it to the Prefs. This has been accordingly done, though he fears fomething too haftily, as he found it proper

to add, while the papers were in
the courfe of printing, fome confiderations on the *Whole* Character
of FALSTAFF; which ought to
have been accompanied by a
flight reform of a few preceding
paffages, which may feem, in confequence of this addition, to contain too favourable a reprefentation
of his Morals.

The vindication of FALSTAFF's
Courage is truly no otherwife the
object than fome old fantaftic Oak,
or grotefque Rock, may be the
object of a morning's ride; yet
being

being propofed as fuch, may ferve
to limit the diftance, and fhape
the courfe : The real object is Exercife, and the Delight which a
rich, beautiful, picturefque, and
perhaps unknown Country, may
excite from every fide. Such an
Exercife may admit of fome little
excurfion, keeping however the Road
in view; but feems to exclude
every appearance of labour and of
toil.—Under the impreffion of fuch
Feelings the Writer has endeavoured to preferve to his Text a
certain lightnefs of air, and chear-

fulnefs

fulnefs of tone; but is fenfible however that the manner of difcuffion does not *every where*, particularly near the commencement, fufficiently correfpond with his defign.—If the Book fhall be fortunate enough to obtain another Impreffion, a feparation may be made; and fuch of the heavier parts as cannot be wholly difpenfed with, fink to their more proper ftation,—a Note.

He is fearful likewife that he may have erred in the other extreme; and that having thought himfelf

himfelf intitled, even in argument, to a certain degree of playful dif-cuffion, may have pufhed it, in a few places, even to levity. This error might be yet more eafily re-formed than the other.—The Book is perhaps, as it ftands, too bulky for the fubject; but if the Reader knew how many preffing confide-rations, as it grew into fize, the Author refifted, which yet feemed intitled to be heard, he would the more readily excufe him.

The whole is a mere Experiment, and the Writer confiders it as fuch :

It

It may have the advantages, but it is likewife attended with all the difficulties and dangers, of *No-velty*.

ON THE

Dramatic Character

OF

Sir *JOHN FALSTAFF.*

THE ideas which I have formed concerning the Courage and Military Character of the Dramatic Sir *John Falstaff*, are so different from those which I find generally to prevail in the world, that I shall take the liberty of stating my sentiments on the subject; in hope that some person as unengaged as myself, will either correct and reform my error in this respect; or, joining himself to my opinion, redeem me from, what I may call, the reproach of singularity.

I am

I am to avow then, that I do not clearly difcern that Sir *John Falftaff* deferves to bear the
character fo generally given him of an abfolute
Coward ; or, in other words, that I do not conceive *Shakefpeare* ever meant to make Cowardice
an effential part of his conftitution.

I know how univerfally the contrary opinion
prevails ; and I know what refpect and deference
are due to the public voice. But if to the avowal
of this fingularity, I add all the reafons that have
led me to it, and acknowledge myfelf to be wholly
in the judgment of the public, I fhall hope to
avoid the cenfure of too much forwardnefs or
indecorum.

It muft, in the firft place, be admitted that the
appearances in this cafe are fingularly ftrong and
ftriking ; and fo they had need be, to become the
ground of fo general a cenfure. We fee this extraordinary Character, almoft in the firft moment
of our acquaintance with him, involved in circumftances

cumftances of apparent difhonour; and we hear him familiarly called *Coward* by his moft intimate companions. We fee him, on occafion of the robbery at *Gads-Hill*, in the very act of running away from the Prince and *Poins*; and we behold him, on another of more honourable obligation, in open day light, in battle, and acting in his profeffion as a Soldier, efcaping from *Douglas* even out of the world as it were; counterfeiting death, and deferting his very exiftence ; and we find him on the former occafion, betrayed into thofe *lies* and *braggadocioes*, which are the ufual concomitants of Cowardice in Military men, and pretenders to valour. Thefe are not only in them-felves ftrong circumftances, but they are more-over thruft forward, preft upon our notice as the fubject of our mirth, as the great bufinefs of the fcene : No wonder, therefore, that the word fhould go forth that *Falftaff* is exhibited as a character of Cowardice and difhonour.

What there is to the contrary of this, it is my bufinefs to difcover. Much, I think, will prefently

appear;

appear; but it lies ſo diſperſed, is ſo latent, and ſo purpoſely obſcured, that the reader muſt have ſome patience whilſt I collect it into one body, and make it the object of a ſteady and regular contemplation.

But what have we to do, may my readers ex-claim, with principles *ſo latent, ſo obſcured?* In Dramatic compoſition the *Impreſſion* is the *Fact*; and the Writer, who, meaning to impreſs one thing, has impreſſed another, is unworthy of obſervation.

It is a very unpleaſant thing to have, in the firſt ſetting out, ſo many and ſo ſtrong prejudices to contend with. All that one can do in ſuch caſe, is, to pray the reader to have a little pati-ence in the commencement; and to reſerve his cenſure, if it muſt paſs, for the concluſion. Under his gracious allowance, therefore, I preſume to declare it, as my opinion, that Cowardice *is not* the *Impreſſion,* which the *whole* character of *Falſtaff*

is

is calculated to make on the minds of an unpre-
judiced audience; tho' there be, I confefs, a
great deal of fomething in the *compofition* likely
enough to puzzle, and confequently to miflead
the Underftanding.—The reader will perceive
that I diftinguifh between *mental Impreffions*, and
the *Underftanding*.—I wifh to avoid every thing
that looks like fubtlety and refinement; but this
is a diftinction, which we all comprehend.—
There are none of us unconfcious of certain feelings or fenfations of mind, which do not feem
to have paffed thro' the Underftanding; the effects,
I fuppofe, of fome fecret influences from without,
acting upon a certain mental fenfe, and producing
feelings and paffions in juft correfpondence to
the force and variety of thofe influences on the
one hand, and to the quicknefs of our fenfibility
on the other. Be the caufe, however, what it may,
the fact is undoubtedly fo; which is all I am
concerned in. And it is equally a fact, which
every man's experience may avouch, that the
Underftanding and thofe feelings are frequently

at variance. The latter often arife from the moft minute circumftances, and frequently from fuch as the Underftanding cannot eftimate, or even re-cognize ; whereas the Underftanding delights in abftraction, and in general propofitions ; which, however true confidered as fuch, are very fel-dom, I had like to have faid *never*, perfectly ap-plicable to any particular cafe. And hence, among other caufes, it is, that we often condemn or applaud characters and actions on the credit of fome logical procefs, while our hearts revolt, and would fain lead us to a very different con-clufion.

The Underftanding feems for the moft part to take cognizance of *actions* only, and from thefe to infer *motives* and *character* ; but the fenfe we have been fpeaking of proceeds in a contrary courfe ; and determines of *actions* from certain *firft principles of character*, which feem wholly out of the reach of the Underftanding. We cannot indeed do otherwife than admit that there muft

be

be diftinct principles of character in every diftinct individual : The manifeft variety even in
the minds of infants will oblige us to this. But
what *are* thefe firft principles of character ?
Not the objects, I am perfuaded, of the Underftanding ; and yet we take as ftrong Impreffions
of them as if we could compare and affort them
in a fyllogifm. We often love or hate at firft
fight ; and indeed, in general, diflike or approve
by fome fecret reference to thefe *principles* ; and
we judge even of conduct, not from any idea
of abftract good or evil in the nature of actions,
but by refering thofe actions to a fuppofed original
character in the man himfelf. I do not mean
that we *talk* thus ; we could not indeed, if we
would, explain ourfelves in detail on this head ;
we can neither account for Impreffions and paffions, nor communicate them to others by *words :*
Tones and looks will fometimes convey the *paffion*
ftrangely, but the *Impreffion* is incommunicable.
The fame caufes may produce it indeed at the fame
time in many, but it is the feparate poffeffion of

each, and not in its nature transferable : It is an imperfect fort of inftinct, and proportionably dumb.—We might indeed, if we chofe it, candidly confefs to one another, that we are greatly fwayed by thefe feelings, and are by no means fo *rational* in all points as we could wifh ; but this would be a betraying of the interefts of that high faculty, the Underftanding, which we fo value ourfelves upon, and which we more peculiarly call our own. This, we think, muft not be ; and fo we huddle up the matter, concealing it as much as pofible, both from ourfelves and others. In Books indeed, wherein character, motive, and action, are all alike fubjected to the Underftanding, it is generally a very clear cafe ; and we make decifions compounded of them all: And thus we are willing to approve of *Candide*, tho' he kills my Lord the Inquifitor, and runs thro' the body the Baron of *Thunder-ten-tronchk* the fon of his patron, and the brother of his beloved *Cunégonde* : But in real life, I believe, *my Lords the Judges* would be apt to inform the

Gentlemen

Gentlemen of the Jury, that my *Lord the Inquifitor* was *ill killed* ; as *Candide* did not proceed on the urgency of the moment, but on the fpeculation only of future evil. And indeed this clear perception, in Novels and Plays, of the union of character and action not feen in nature, is the principal defect of fuch compofitions, and what renders them but ill pictures of human life, and wretched guides of conduct.

But if there was *one man* in the world, who could make a more perfect draught of real nature, and fteal fuch Impreffions on his audience, without their fpecial notice, as fhould keep their hold in fpite of any error of their Underftanding, and fhould thereupon venture to introduce an apparent incongruity of character and action, for ends which I fhall prefently endeavour to explain ; fuch an imitation would be worth our niceft curiofity and attention. But in fuch a cafe as this, the reader might expect that he fhould find us all talking the language of the Under-

ftanding

ftanding only ; that is, cenfuring the action with very little confcientious inveftigation even of *that* ; and transferring the cenfure, in every odi-ous colour, to the actor himfelf ; how much fo-ever our hearts and affections might fecretly revolt : For as to the *Impreſſion*, we have already obferved that it has no tongue ; nor is its operation and influence likely to be made the fubject of conference and communication.

It is not to the *Courage* only of *Falſtaff* that we think thefe obfervations will apply : No part whatever of his character feems to be fully fettled in our minds ; at leaft there is fomething ftrangely incongruous in our difcourfe and affections concerning him. We all like *Old Jack* ; yet, by fome ftrange perverfe fate, we all abufe him, and deny him the poffeffion of any one fingle good or refpectable quality. There is fomething extraordinary in this : It muft be a ftrange art in *Shakeſpeare* which can draw our liking and good will towards fo offenfive an object. He has wit, it will be faid ; chearfulnefs and hu-mour of the moft characteriftic and captivating

fort

fort. And is this enough ? Is the humour and gaiety of vice fo very captivating ? Is the wit, characteriftic of bafenefs and every ill quality capable of attaching the heart and winning the affections ? Or does not the apparency of fuch humour, and the flafhes of fuch wit, by more ftrongly difclofing the deformity of character, but the more effectually excite our hatred and contempt of the man ? And yet this is not our *feeling* of *Falftaff*'s character. When he has ceafed to amufe us, we find no emotions of difguft ; we can fcarcely forgive the ingratitude of the Prince in the new-born virtue of the King, and we curfe the feverity of that poetic juftice which configns our old good-natured delightful companion to the cuftody of the *warden*, and the difhonours of the *Fleet.*

I am willing, however, to admit that if a Dramatic writer will but preferve to any character the qualities of a ftrong mind, particularly Courage and ability, that it will be afterwards no very difficult tafk (as I may have occafion to explain)

plain) to difcharge that *difguft* which arifes from
vicious manners ; and even to attach us (if fuch
character fhould contain any quality productive
of chearfulnefs and laughter) to the caufe and
fubject of our mirth with fome degree of affection.

But the queftion which I am to confider is of
a very different nature : It is a queftion of fact,
and concerning a quality which forms the bafis of
every refpectable character ; a quality which
is the very effence of a Military man ; and which
is held up to us, in almoft every Comic incident
of the Play, as the fubject of our obfervation.
It is ftrange then that it fhould now be a queftion,
whether *Falftaff* is, or is not a man of Courage;
and whether we do in fact contemn him for the
want, or refpect him for the poffeffion of that
quality :   And yet I believe the reader will find
that he has by no means decided this queftion,
even for himfelf.—If then it fhould turn out,
that this difficulty has arifen out of the Art of

Shakefpeare

Shakespeare, who has contrived to make secret Impressions upon us of Courage, and to preserve those Impressions in favour of a character which was to be held up for sport and laughter on account of actions of apparent Cowardice and dishonour, we shall have less occasion to wonder, as *Shakespeare* is a Name which contains All of Dramatic artifice and genius.

If in this place the reader shall peevishly and prematurely object that the observations and distinctions I have laboured to establish, are wholly unapplicable; he being himself unconscious of ever having received any such Impression; what can be done in so nice a case, but to refer him to the following pages; by the number of which he may judge how very much I respect his objection, and by the variety of those proofs, which I shall employ to induce him to part with it; and to recognize in its stead certain feelings, concealed and covered over perhaps, but not erazed, by time, reasoning, and authority.

In

In the mean while, it may not perhaps be
eafy for him to refolve how it comes about,
that, whilft we look upon *Falftaff* as a character
of the like nature with that of *Parolles* or of *Bobadil*, we fhould preferve for him a great degree
of refpect and good-will, and yet feel the higheft
difdain and contempt of the others, tho' they are
all involved in fimilar fituations. The reader,
I believe, would wonder extremely to find either
Parolles or *Bobadil* poffefs himfelf in danger:
What then can be the caufe that we are not at
all furprized at the gaiety and eafe of *Falftaff* under the moft trying circumftances; and that
we never think of charging *Shakefpeare* with de-
parting, on this account, from the truth and coherence of character? Perhaps, after all, the
real character of *Falftaff* may be different from
his *apparent* one; and poffibly this difference
between reality and appearance, whilft it accounts
at once for our liking and our cenfure, may be
the true point of humour in the character, and
the fource of all our laughter and delight. We

may

may chance to find, if we will but examine a little into the nature of thofe circumftances which have accidentally involved him, that he was intended to be drawn as a character of much Natural courage and refolution; and be obliged thereupon to repeal thofe decifions, which may have been made upon the credit of fome general tho' unapplicable propofitions; the common fource of error in other and higher matters. A little reflection may perhaps bring us round again to the point of our departure, and unite our Underftandings to our inftinct.—Let us then for a moment *fufpend* at leaft our decifions, and candidly and coolly inquire if Sir *John Falftaff* be, indeed, what he has fo often been called by critic and commentator, male and female,—a *Conftitutional Coward.*

It will fcarcely be poffible to confider the Courage of *Falftaff* as wholly detached from his other qualities: But I write not profeffedly of any part of his character, but what is included under the

term

term, *Courage* ; however I may incidentally throw fome lights on the whole.—The reader will not need to be told that this Inquiry will refolve itfelf of courfe into a Critique on the genius, the arts, and the conduct of *Shakefpeare :* For what is *Falftaff,* what *Lear,* what *Hamlet,* or *Othello,* but different modifications of *Shakefpeare*'s thought? It is true that this Inquiry is narrowed almoft to a fingle point : But general criticifm is as uninftructive as it is eafy : *Shakefpeare* deferves to be confidered in detail ;—a tafk hitherto unattempted.

It may be proper, in the firft place, to take a fhort view of all the parts of *Falftaff*'s Character, and then proceed to difcover, if we can, what *Impreffions,* as to Courage or Cowardice, he had made on the perfons of the Drama : After which we will examine, in courfe, fuch evidence, either of *perfons* or *facts,* as are relative to the matter ; and account as we may for thofe appearances, which feem to have led to the opinion of his Conftitutional Cowardice.   The

The fcene of the robbery, and the difgraces attending it, which ftand firft in the Play, and introduce us to the knowledge of *Falftaff*, I fhall beg leave (as I think this fcene to have been the fource of much unreafonable prejudice) to *referve* till we are more fully acquainted with the whole chara&er of *Falftaff*; and I fhall therefore hope that the reader will not for a time advert to it, or to the jefts of the *Prince* or of *Poins* in confequence of that unlucky adventure.

In drawing out the parts of *Falftaff*'s chara&er, with which I fhall begin this Inquiry, I fhall take the liberty of putting Conftitutional bravery into his compofition ; but the reader will be pleafed to confider what I fhall fay in that refpe& as fpoken hypothetically for the prefent, to be retained, or difcharged out of it, as he fhall finally determine.

To me then it appears that the leading quality in *Falftaff*'s chara&er, and that from which all the reft take their colour, is a high degree of wit

C   and

and humour, accompanied with great natural vigour and alacrity of mind. This quality fo accompanied, led him probably very early into life, and made him highly acceptable to fociety; fo acceptable, as to make it feem unneceffary for him to acquire any other virtue. Hence, perhaps, his continued debaucheries and diffipations of every kind.—He feems, by nature, to have had a mind free of malice or any evil principle ; but he never took the trouble of acquiring any good one. He found himfelf efteemed and beloved with all his faults; nay *for* his faults, which were all connected with humour, and for the moft part, grew out of it. As he had, poffibly, no vices but fuch as he thought might be openly profeffed, fo he appeared more diffolute thro' oftentation. To the character of wit and humour, to which all his other qualities feem to have conformed themfelves, he appears to have added a very neceffary fupport, *that* of the profeffion of a *Soldier*. He had from nature, as I prefume to fay, a fpirit of boldnefs and enterprife ; which in a Military

age,

age, tho' employment was only occafional, kept him always above contempt, fecured him an honourable reception among the Great, and fuited beft both with his particular mode of humour and of vice. Thus living continually in fociety, nay even in Taverns, and indulging himfelf, and being indulged by others, in every debauchery; drinking, whoring, gluttony, and eafe; affuming a liberty of fiction, neceffary perhaps to his wit, and often falling into falfity and lies, he feems to have fet, by degrees, all fober reputation at defiance; and finding eternal refources in his wit, he borrows, fhifts, defrauds, and even robs, without difhonour.—Laughter and approbation attend his greateft exceffes; and being governed vifibly by no fettled bad principle or ill defign, fun and humour account for and cover all. By degrees, however, and thro' indulgence, he acquires bad habits, becomes an humourift, grows enormoufly corpulent, and falls into the infirmities of age; yet never quits, all the time, one fingle levity or vice of youth, or lofes any of that chearfulnefs of

C 2   mind,

mind, which had enabled him to pafs thro' this
courfe with eafe to himfelf and delight to others;
and thus, at laft, mixing youth and age, enterprize and corpulency, wit and folly, poverty and
expence, title and buffoonery, innocence as to
purpofe, and wickednefs as to practice; neither
incurring hatred by bad principle, or contempt
by Cowardice, yet involved in circumftances productive of imputation in both; a butt and a wit,
a humourift and a man of humour, a touchftone
and a laughing ftock, a jefter and a jeft, has Sir
John Falftaff, taken at that period of his life in
which we fee him, become the moft perfect Comic character that perhaps ever was exhibited.

It may not poffibly be wholly amifs to remark
in this place, that if Sir *John Falftaff* had poffeffed
any of that Cardinal quality, Prudence, alike the
guardian of virtue and the protector of vice;
that quality, from the poffeffion or the abfence
of which, the character and fate of men in this
life take, I think, their colour, and not from real
vice or virtue; if he had confidered his wit not as
principal but *acceffary* only; as the inftrument of

power, and not as power itfelf; if he had had much
bafenefs to hide, if he had had lefs of what may
be called mellownefs or good humour, or lefs of
health and fpirit; if he had fpurred and rode the
world with his wit, inftead of fuffering the world,
boys and all, to ride him;—he might, without
any other effential change, have been the admiration and not the jeft of mankind :—Or if he
had lived in our day, and inftead of attaching
himfelf to one Prince, had renounced *all* friend-
fhip and *all* attachment, and had let himfelf out
as the ready inftrument and Zany of every fuccef-
five Minifter, he might poffibly have acquired
the high honour of marking his fhroud or deco-
rating his coffin with the living rays of an Irifh
at leaft, if not a Britifh Coronet : Inftead of
which, tho' enforcing laughter from every difpofition, he appears, now, as fuch a character,
which every wife man will pity and avoid, every
knave will cenfure, and every fool will fear : And
accordingly *Shakefpeare*, ever true to nature, has
made *Harry* defert, and *Lancafter* cenfure him :
—He dies where he lived, in a Tavern, broken-

hearted, without a friend ; and his final exit is given up to the derifion of fools. Nor has his misfortunes ended here; the fcandal arifing from the mifapplication of his wit and talents feems immortal. He has met with as little juftice or mercy from his final judges the critics, as from his companions of the Drama. With our cheeks ftill red with laughter, we ungratefully as unjuftly cenfure him as a coward by nature, and a rafcal upon principle : Tho', if this were fo, it might be hoped, for our own credit, that we fhould behold him rather with difguft and difapprobation than with pleafure and delight.

But to remember our queftion—*Is Falftaff a conftitutional coward ?*

With refpect to every infirmity, except that of Cowardice, we muft take him as at the period in which he is reprefented to us. If we fee him diffipated, fat,—it is enough ;—we have nothing to do with his youth, when he might perhaps

have

have been modeſt, chaſte, "*and not an Eagle's talon in the waiſt.*" But *Conſtitutional Courage* extends to a man's whole life, makes a part of his nature, and is not to be taken up or deſerted like a mere Moral quality. It is true, there is a Courage founded upon *principle*, or rather a principle independent of Courage, which will ſometimes operate in ſpite of nature ; a principle, which prefers death to ſhame, but which always refers itſelf, in conformity to its own nature, to the prevailing modes of honour, and the faſhions of the age.—But Natural courage is another thing : It is independent of opinion ; It adapts itſelf to occaſions, preſerves itſelf under every ſhape, and can avail itſelf of flight as well as of action.—In the laſt war, ſome Indians of America perceiving a line of Highlanders to keep their ſtation under every diſadvantage, and under a fire which they could not effectually return, were ſo miſerably miſtaken in our points of honour as to conjecture, from obſervation on the habit and ſtability of thoſe troops, that they were indeed the women of England, who wanted courage to run away.—That Courage which is founded in nature and conſtitution, *Falſtaff*, as I preſume to ſay, poſſeſſed ;—but I am ready to allow, that the principle already mentioned, ſo far as it refers to reputation only, began with every other Moral quality to loſe its hold on him in his old age ; that is, at the time of life in which he is repreſented to us ; a period, as it ſhould ſeem, approaching to *ſeventy*.—The truth is that he had drollery enough to ſupport himſelf in credit without the point of honour, and had addreſs enough to make even the preſervation of his life a point of drollery. The reader knows I allude, tho' ſomething prematurely, to his fictitious death in the battle of Shrewſbury. This incident is generally conſtrued to the diſadvantage of *Falſtaff :* It is a tranſaction which bears the external marks of Cowardice : It is alſo aggravated to the ſpectators by the idle tricks of the Player, who practiſes

on

on this occasion all the attitudes and wild ap-
prehensions of fear; more ambitious, as it should
seem, of representing a Caliban than a *Falstaff*;
or indeed rather a poor unweildy miserable Tor-
toise than either.—The painful Comedian lies
spread out on his belly, and not only covers himself all over with his robe as with a shell, but
forms a kind of round Tortoise-back by I know
not what stuffing or contrivance; in addition to
which, he alternately lifts up, and depresses, and
dodges his head, and looks to the one side and to
the other, so much with the piteous aspect of that
animal, that one would not be sorry to see the ambitious imitator calipashed in his robe, and served
up for the entertainment of the gallery.—There
is no hint for this mummery in the Play : Whatever there may be of dishonour in *Falstaff*'s conduct, he neither does or says any thing on this
occasion which indicates terror or disorder of
mind : On the contrary, this very act is a
proof of his having all his wits about him, and
is a stratagem, such as it is, not improper for a

buffoon

buffoon, whofe fate would be fingularly hard, if he fhould not be allowed to avail himfelf of his Character when it might ferve him in moft ftead. We muft remember, in extenuation, that the executive, the deftroying hand of *Douglas* was over him : " *It was time to counterfeit, or that* " *hot termagant Scot had paid him fcot and lot too.*" He had but one choice ; he was obliged to pafs thro' the ceremony of dying either in jeft or in earneft ; and we fhall not be furprized at the event, when we remember his propenfities to the former.—Life (and efpecially the life of *Falftaff*) might be a jeft ; but he could fee no joke what- ever in dying : To be chopfallen was, with him, to lofe both life and character together : He faw the point of honour, as well as every thing elfe, in ridiculous lights, and began to renounce its tyranny.

But I am too much in advance, and muft retreat for more advantage. I fhould not for- get how much opinion is againft me, and that I am to make my way by the mere force and

weight

weight of evidence ; without which I muſt not hope to poſſeſs myſelf of the reader : No addreſs, no inſinuation will avail. To this evidence, then, I now reſort. The Courage of *Falſtaff* is my Theme: And no paſſage will I ſpare from which any thing can be inferred as relative to this point. It would be as vain as injudicious to attempt con-cealment : How could I eſcape detection ? The Play is in every one's memory, and a ſingle paſ-ſage remembered in detection would tell, in the mind of the partial obſerver, for fifty times its real weight. Indeed this argument would be void of all excuſe if it declined any difficulty ; if it did not meet, if it did not challenge oppoſition. Every paſſage then ſhall be produced from which, in my opinion, any inference, favourable or unfavourable, has or can be drawn ;—but not methodically, not formally, as texts for comment, but as chance or convenience ſhall lead the way ; but in what ſhape ſoever, they ſhall be always diſtinguiſhingly marked for notice. And ſo

with

with that attention to truth and candour which
ought to accompany even our lighteft amufements
I proceed to offer fuch proof as the cafe will admit, that *Courage* is a part of *Falftaff's Character*,
that it belonged to his conftitution, and was manifeft in the conduct and practice of his whole
life.

Let us then examine, as a fource of very authentic information, what Impreffions *Sir John
Falftaff* had made on the characters of the Drama;
and in what eftimation he is fuppofed to ftand
with mankind in general as to the point of Perfonal Courage. But the quotations we make for this
or other purpofes, muft, it is confeffed, be lightly
touched, and no particular paffage ftrongly re-
lied on, either in his favour or againft him.
Every thing which he himfelf fays, or is faid of
him, is fo phantaftically difcoloured by humour,
or folly, or jeft, that we muft for the moft part
look to the fpirit rather than the letter of what

is

is uttered, and rely at laſt only on a combination of the whole.

We will begin then, if the reader pleaſes, by inquiring what Impreſſion the very Vulgar had taken of *Falſtaff.* If it is not that of Cowardice, be it what elſe it may, that of a man of violence, or *a Ruffian in years,* as Harry calls him, or any thing elſe, it anſwers my purpoſe; how inſignificant ſoever the characters or incidents to be firſt produced may otherwiſe appear;—for theſe Impreſſions muſt have been taken either from perſonal knowledge and obſervation; or, what will do better for my purpoſe, from common fame. Altho' I muſt admit ſome part of this evidence will appear ſo weak and trifling that it certainly ought not to be produced but in proof Impreſſion only.

The *Hoſteſs Quickly* employs two officers to arreſt *Falſtaff*: On the mention of his name, one of them immediately obſerves, "*that it may chance to coſt ſome*

"*of*

"*of them their lives, for that he will ſtab.—Alas a day,*"
ſays the hoſteſs, "*take heed of him, he cares not*
"*what miſchief he doth*; *if his weapon be out he will*
"*foin like any devil*; *He will ſpare neither man,*
"*woman, or child.*" Accordingly, we find that
when they lay hold on him he reſiſts to the utmoſt
of his power, and calls upon *Bardolph*, whoſe
arms are at liberty, to draw. "*Away, varlets, draw*
"*Bardolph, cut me off the villain's head, throw the*
quean in the kennel." The officers cry, *a reſcue, a*
reſcue ! But the Chief Juſtice comes in and the
ſcuffle ceaſes. In another ſcene, his wench *Doll*
Tearſheet aſks him "*when he will leave fighting*
* * * * * * *and patch up his old body for heaven.*"
This is occaſioned by his drawing his rapier, on
great provocation, and driving *Piſtol*, who is
drawn likewiſe, down ſtairs, and hurting him in
the ſhoulder. To drive *Piſtol* was no great feat;
nor do I mention it as ſuch ; but upon this
occaſion it was neceſſary. "*A Raſcal bragging ſlave,*
ſays he, "*the rogue fled from me like quickſilver.*" Ex-
preſſions, which as they remember the cowardice

ardice of *Piſtol*, ſeem to prove that *Falſtaff* did not value himſelf on the adventure. Even ſomething may be drawn from *Davy, Shallow's* ſerving man, who calls *Falſtaff,* in ignorant admiration, the *man of war.* I muſt obſerve here, and I beg the reader will notice it, that there is not a ſingle expreſſion dropt by theſe people, or either of *Falſtaff*'s followers, from which may be inferred the leaſt ſuſpicion of Cowardice in his character; and this is I think ſuch an *implied negation* as deſerves conſiderable weight.

But to go a little higher, if, indeed, to conſider *Shallow's* opinion be to go *higher*: It is from him, however, that we get the earlieſt account of Falſtaff. He *remembers him a Page to Thomas Mowbray Duke of Norfolk :* "*He broke,* ſays he, "*Schoggan's head at the Court-Gate when he was* " *but a crack thus high.*" *Shallow,* throughout, conſiders him as a great Leader and Soldier, and relates this fact as an early indication only of his future Prowefs. *Shallow* it is true, is a very ridiculous

culous character; but he picked up thefe Impreffions fomewhere; and he picked up none of
a contrary tendency.—I want at prefent only to
prove that *Falftaff* ftood well in the report of common fame as to this point; and he was now near
feventy years of age, and had paffed in a Military
line thro' the active part of his life. At this
period common fame may be well confidered as
the *feal* of his character; a feal which ought not
perhaps to be broke open on the evidence of any
future tranfaction.

But to proceed. *Lord Bardolph* was a man of
the world, and of fenfe and obfervation. He in-
forms *Northumberland*, erroneoufly indeed, that
Percy had beaten the King at Shrewfbury. " *The
King*," according to him, " *was wounded; the
" Prince of Wales and the two Blunts flain, certain
" Nobles*, whom he names, *had efcaped by flight, and
" the Brawn Sir John Falftaff was taken prifoner.*"
But how came *Falftaff* into this lift? Common
fame had put him there. He is fingularly obli-
                                                    ged

ged to Common fame.—But if he had not been a Soldier of repute, if he had not been brave as well as fat, if he had been *mere brawn*, it would have been more germane to the matter if this lord had put him down among the baggage or the provender. The fact feems to be, that there is a real confequence about Sir *John Falftaff* which is not brought forward : We fee him only in his familiar hours ; we enter the tavern with *Hal* and *Poins*; we join in the laugh and *take a pride to gird at him :* But there may be a great deal of truth in what he himfelf writes to the Prince, that tho' he be "*Jack Falftaff with his Familiars, he is* Sir John *with the reft of Europe.*" It has been re-marked, and very truly I believe, that no man is a hero in the eye of his valet-de-chambre ; and *thus* it is, we are witneffes only of *Falftaff*'s weak-nefs and buffoonery; our acquaintance is with *Jack Falftaff, Plump Jack,* and *Sir John Paunch*; but if we would look for *Sir John Falftaff*, we muft put on, as *Bunyan* would have expreffed it, the fpecta-cles of obfervation. With refpect, for inftance,

D

to his Military command at Shrewſbury, nothing appears on the ſurface but the Prince's familiarly ſaying, in the tone uſually aſſumed when ſpeaking of *Falſtaff*, "*I will procure this fat rogue a Charge* "*of foot* ;" and in another place, "*I will procure* "*thee Jack a Charge of foot*; *meet me to-morrow in the* "*Temple Hall*." Indeed we might venture to infer from this, that a Prince of ſo great ability, whoſe wildneſs was only external and aſſumed, would not have procured, in ſo nice and critical a conjuncture, a Charge of foot for a known Coward. But there was more it ſeems in the caſe : We now find from this report, to which *Lord Bardolph* had given full credit, that the world had its eye upon *Falſtaff* as an officer of merit, whom it expected to find in the field, and whoſe fate in the battle was an object of Public concern : His life was, it ſeems, very material indeed ; a thread of ſo much dependence, that *fiction*, weaving the fates of Princes, did not think it unworthy, how coarſe ſoever, of being made a part of the tiſſue.

We

We fhall next produce the evidence of the Chief Juftice of England. He inquires of his attendant, " *if the man who was then paffing him was* " Falftaff; *he who was in queftion for the robbery.*" The attendant anfwers affirmatively, but reminds his lord " *that he had fince done good fervice at Shrewfbury;* " and the Chief Juftice, on this occafion, rating him for his debaucheries, tells him " *that his day's fervice at Shrewfbury had gilded over* " *his night's exploit at Gads Hill.*" This is furely more than Common fame: *The Chief Juftice* muft have known his whole character taken together, and muft have received the moft authentic information, and in the trueft colours, of his behaviour in that action.

But, perhaps, after all, the Military men may be efteemed the beft judges in points of this nature. Let us hear then *Coleville* of the dale, *a Soldier, in degree a Knight, a famous rebel, and* " *whofe* " *betters, had they been ruled by him, would have fold* " *themfelves dearer:*" A man who is of confequence

enough

enough to be guarded by *Blunt* and *led to prefent execution.* This man yields himfelf up even to the very Name and Reputation of *Falftaff.* "*I think,*" fays he, "*you are Sir John Falftaff, and in that thought* "*yield me.*" But this is but one only among the men of the fword ; they fhall be produced then by *dozens,* if that will fatisfy. Upon the return of the King and Prince Henry from Wales, the Prince feeks out and finds *Falftaff* debauching in a tavern ; where *Peto* prefently brings an account of ill news from the North ; and adds, "*that as he came along he met or overtook a dozen Captains, bare headed, fweating, knocking at the taverns, and afking every one for* Sir John Falftaff. He is followed by *Bardolph,* who informs *Falftaff* that "*He muft away* "*to the Court immediately*; *a dozen Captains ftay at* "*door for him.*" Here is Military evidence in abundance, and *Court evidence* too ; for what are we to infer from *Falftaff*'s being fent for to Court on this ill news, but that his opinion was to be afked, as a Military man of fkill and experience, concerning the defences necefsary to be taken. Nor is

Shakefpeare

Shakeſpeare content, here, with leaving us to gather up *Falſtaff*'s *better charaƈter* from inference and deduƈtion : He comments on the faƈt by making *Falſtaff* obſerve that "*Men of merit are ſought after:* "*The undeſerver may ſleep when the man of aƈtion is* "*called on.*" I do not wiſh to draw *Falſtaff*'s charaƈter out of his own mouth ; but this obſervation refers to the faƈt, and is founded in reaſon. Nor ought we to rejeƈt, what in another place he ſays to the Chief Juſtice, as it is in the nature of an appeal to his knowledge. "*There is not a dan-* "*gerous aƈtion,*" ſays he, "*can peep out his head but I am thruſt upon it.*" The Chief Juſtice ſeems by his anſwer to admit the faƈt. "*Well, be honeſt, be honeſt, and heaven bleſs your expedition.*" But the whole paſſage may deſerve tranſcribing.

Ch. Juſt. "*Well, the King has ſevered you and Prince Henry. I hear you are going with Lord John of Lancaſter, againſt the Archbiſhop and the Earl of Northumberland.*"

"*Falf. Yes, I thank your pretty sweet wit for it; but*
" *look you pray, all you that kiss my lady peace at home,*
" *that our armies join not in a hot day ; for I take but*
" *two shirts out with me, and I mean not to sweat ex-*
" *traordinarily : If it be a hot day, if I brandish any*
" *thing but a bottle, would I might never spit white*
" *again.   There is not a dangerous action can peep*
" *out his head but I am thrust upon it.   Well I cannot*
" *last for ever.—But it was always the trick of our*
" *English nation, if they have a good thing to make it*
" *too common.   If you will needs say I am an old man*
" *you should give me rest : I would to God my name*
" *were not so terrible to the enemy as it is.   I were*
" *better to be eaten to death with a rust than to be scour'd*
" *to nothing with perpetual motion.*"

"Ch. Juft. *Well be honest, be honest, and heaven*
" *bless your expedition.*"

Falstaff indulges himfelf here in humourous
exaggeration ;—thefe paffages are not meant to
be taken, nor are we to fuppofe that they were
taken

taken, literally;—but if there was not a ground
of truth, if *Falſtaff* had not had ſuch a degree of
Military reputation as was capable of being thus
humourouſly amplified and exaggerated, the
whole dialogue would have been highly prepoſ-
terous and abſurd, and the acquieſcing anſwer of
the *Lord Chief Juſtice* ſingularly improper.—But
upon the ſuppoſition of *Falſtaff*'s being conſidered, upon the whole, as a good and gallant Officer,
the anſwer is juſt, and correſponds with the acknowledgment which had a little before been
made, "*that his day's ſervice at Shrewſbury had gilded*
"*over his night's exploit at Gads Hill.—You may*
"*thank the unquiet time*, ſays the Chief Juſtice,
"*for your quiet o'erpoſting of that action ;*" agreeing
with what *Falſtaff* ſays in another place ;—"*Well*
"*God be thanked for theſe Rebels, they offend none but*
"*the virtuous ; I laud them, I praiſe them.*"—Whether this be ſaid in the true ſpirit of a Soldier or
not, I do not determine ; it is ſurely not in that
of a mere Coward and Poltroon.

It will be needlefs to fhew, which might be done from a variety of particulars, that *Falſtaff* was known, and had confideration at Court. *Shallow* cultivates him in the idea that *a friend at Court is better than a penny in purſe*: *Weſtmorland* fpeaks to him in the tone of an equal : Upon *Falſtaff's* telling him, that he thought his lordſhip had been already at Shrewſbury, *Weſtmorland* replies,—*Faith Sir John, 'tis more than time* " *that I were there, and you too* ; *the King I can tell* " *you looks for us all* ; *we muſt away all to night.*— " *Tut,* fays Falſtaff, *never fear me, I am as vigilant* " *as a cat to ſteal cream.*"—He defires, in another place, of my lord John of Lancaſter, " *that when he goes to Court, he may ſtand in his good report.*" His intercourſe and correſpondence with both thefe lords feem eafy and familiar. *Go,* fays he to the page, " *bear this to my Lord of Lancaſter, this* " *to the Prince, this to the Earl of Weſtmorland, and* " *this* (for he extended himſelf on all fides) *to old Mrs. Urſula,*" whom it feems, the rogue ought to have married many years before.—But thefe

intimations

intimations are needlefs : We fee him ourfelves in the *Royal Prefence*; where, certainly, his buffooneries never brought him ; nor was the Prince of a character to commit fo high an indecorum, as to thruft, upon a folemn occafion, a mere Tavern companion into his father's Prefence, efpecially in a moment when he himfelf deferts his loofer character, and takes up that of *a Prince indeed*. —In a very important fcene, where *Worcefter* is expected with propofals from *Percy*, and wherein he is received, is treated with, and carries back offers of accomodation from the King, the King's attendants upon the occafion are *the Prince of Wales, Lord John of Lancafter, the Earl of Weftmorland, Sir Walter Blunt, and Sir John Falftaff.*—What fhall be faid to this ? Falftaff is not furely introduced here in vicious indulgence to a mob audience ;—he utters but one word, a buffoon one indeed, but afide and to the Prince only. Nothing, it fhould feem, is wanting, if decorum would here have permitted, but that he fhould have fpoken one fober fentence in the

Prefence

Prefence (which yet we are to fuppofe him ready
and able to do if occafion fhould have required;
or his wit was given him to little purpofe) and
Sir *John Falſtaff* might be allowed to paſs for an
eftablifhed Courtier and counfellor of ſtate. " *If*
" *I do grow great,* fays he, *I'll grow leſs, purge and*
" *leave ſack, and live as a nobleman ſhould do.*" Nobility did not then appear to him at an unmea-
furable diftance; it was, it feems, in his idea,
the very next link in the chain.

But to return. I would now demand what could
bring *Falſtaff* into the Royal Prefence upon fuch
an occafion, or juftify the Prince's fo public acknowledgment of him, but an eftablifhed fame
and reputation of Military merit? In fhort, juft
the like merit as brought Sir *Walter Blunt* into
the fame circumftances of honour.

But it may be objected that his introduction
into this fcene is a piece of indecorum in the
author. But upon what ground are we to fup-

pofe

pofe this ? Upon the ground of his being a no-
torious Coward ? Why this is the very point in
queftion, and cannot be granted: Even the direct
contrary I have affirmed, and am endeavouring
to fupport. But if it be fuppofed upon any other
ground, it does not concern me; I have nothing
to do with *Shakefpeare*'s indecorums in general.
That there are indecorums in the Play I have no
doubt: The indecent treatment of *Percy*'s dead
body is the greateft ;—the familiarity of the infig-
nificant, rude, and even ill difpofed *Poins* with the
Prince, is another ;—but the admiffion of *Falftaff*
into the Royal Prefence (fuppofing, which I have
a right to fuppofe, that his Military character
was unimpeached) does not feem to be in any
refpect among the number. In camps there is
but one virtue and one vice ; Military merit
fwallows up or covers all. But, after all, what
have we to do with indecorums ? Indecorums refpect the propriety or impropriety of exhibiting
certain actions ;—not their *truth* or *falfhood* when
exhibited. *Shakefpeare* ftands to us in the place

of

of *truth* and *nature*: If we defert this principle we cut the turf from under us; I may then object to the robbery and other paffages as indecorums, and as contrary to the truth of character. In fhort we may rend and tear the Play to pieces, and every man carry off what fentences he likes beft.—But why this inveterate malice againft poor *Falftaff?* He has faults enough in confcience without loading him with the infamy of Cowardice; a charge, which, if true, would, if I am not greatly miftaken, fpoil all our mirth.—But of that hereafter.

It feems to me that, in our hafty judgment of fome particular tranfactions, we forget the circumftances and condition of his whole life and character, which yet deferve our very particular attention. The author, it is true, has thrown the moft advantageous of thefe circumftances into the *back ground* as it were, and has brought nothing *out of the canvafs* but his follies and buffoonery. We difcover however, that in a very early period

of

of his life he was familiar with *John* of *Gaunt*; which could hardly be, unlefs he had poffeffed much perfonal gallantry and accomplifhment, and had derived his birth from a diftinguifhed at leaft, if not from a Noble family.

It may feem very extravagant to infift upon *Falftaff*'s birth as a ground from which, by any inference, Perfonal courage may be derived, efpecially after having acknowledged that he feemed to have deferted thofe points of honour, which are more peculiarly the accompanyments of rank. But it may be obferved that in the Feudal ages rank and wealth were not only connected with the point of honour, but with perfonal ftrength and natural courage. It is obfervable that Courage is a quality, which is at leaft as tranfmiffible to one's pofterity as features and complexion. In thefe periods men acquired and maintained their rank and poffeffions by perfonal prowefs and gallantry; and their marriage alliances were made, of courfe, in families of the

fame

fame character : And from hence, and from the
exercifes of their youth, we muft account for the
diftinguifhed force and bravery of our antient
Barons. It is not therefore befide my purpofe
to inquire what hints of the origin and birth of
Falftaff, *Shakefpeare* may have dropped in different
parts of the Play ; for tho' we may be difpofed
to allow that *Falftaff* in his old age might, under
particular influences, defert the point of honour,
we cannot give up that unalienable poffeffion
of Courage, which might have been derived to
him from a noble or diftinguifhed ftock.

But it may be faid that *Falftaff* was in truth the
child of invention only, and that a reference to
the Feudal accidents of birth ferves only to confound fiction with reality : Not altogether fo.
If the ideas of Courage and *birth* were ftrongly
affociated in the days of *Shakefpeare*, then would
the affignment of high birth to *Falftaff* carry, and
be intended to carry along with it, to the minds
of the audience the affociated idea of Courage,

if

if nothing fhould be fpecially interpofed to dif-
folve the connection ;—and the queftion is as
concerning this intention, and this effect.

I fhall proceed yet farther to make a few very
minute obfervations of the fame nature : But
if *Shakefpeare* meant fometimes rather to *imprefs*
than explain, no circumftances calculated to this
end, either directly or by affociation, are too minute
for notice. But however this may be, a more con-
ciliating reafon ftill remains : The argument itfelf, like the tales of our Novelifts, is a *vehicle*
only; *theirs*, as they profefs, of moral inftruction;
and *mine* of critical amufement. The vindication
of *Falftaff*'s Courage deferves not for its own fake
the leaft fober difcuffion; *Falftaff* is the word only,
Shakefpeare is the *Theme :* And if thro' this channel, I can furnifh no irrational amufement, the
reader will not, perhaps, every where expect from
me the ftrict feverity of logical inveftigation.

Falftaff, then, it may be obferved, was introduced into the world,—(at leaft we are told fo)
by

by the name of *Oldcaftle*.* This was affigning him an origin of nobility; but the family of that name difclaiming any kindred with his vices, he was thereupon, as it is faid, ingrafted into another ftock† fcarcely lefs diftinguifhed, tho' fallen into indelible difgraces; and by this means

---

I believe the ftage was in poffeffion of fome rude outline of *Falftaff* before the time of *Shakefpeare*, under the name of *Sir John Oldcaftle*; and I think it probable that this name was retained for a period in *Shakefpeare*'s Hen. 4th. but changed to *Falftaff* before the play was printed. The expreffion of "*Old Lad of the Caftle*," ufed by the Prince, does not however decidedly prove this; as it might have been only fome known and familiar appellation too carelefly transferred from the old Play.

† I doubt if *Shakefpeare* had Sir *John Faftolfe* in his memory when he called the character under confideration *Falftaff*. The title and name of *Sir John* were transferred from *Oldcaftle* not *Faftolfe*, and there is no kind of fimilarity in the characters. If he had *Faftolfe* in his thought at all, it was that while he approached the name, he might make fuch a departure from it as the difference of character feemed to require

he

he has been made, if the conjectures of certain critics are well founded, the Dramatic fucceffor, tho', having refpect to chronology, the natural *proavus* of another Sir *John*, who was no lefs than a Knight of the moft noble order of the Garter, but a name for ever difhonoured by a frequent expofure in that Drum-and-trumpet Thing called *The firft part of Henry* VI. written doubtlefs, or rather exhibited, long before *Shakefpeare* was born,* tho' afterwards repaired, I think, and

E   furbifhed

---

* It would be no difficult matter I think to prove that all thofe Plays taken from the Englifh chronicle, which are afcribed to *Shakefpeare*, were on the ftage before his time, and that he was employed by the Players only to refit and repair, taking due care to retain the names of the characters and to preferve all thofe incidents which were the moft popular. Some of thefe Plays, particularly the two parts of Hen. IV. have certainly received what may be called a *thorough repair*; that is, *Shakefpeare* new-wrote them to the old names. In the latter part of Hen. V. fome of the old materials remain; and in the Play which I have here cenfured (Hen. VI.) we fee very little of the new. I fhould conceive it would not be very difficult to feel one's

way

furbiſhed up by him with here and there a little
ſentiment and diction. This family, if any
branch

way thro' theſe Plays, and diſtinguiſh every where
the metal from the clay. Of the two Plays of Hen.
IV. there has been, I have admitted, a complete
tranſmutation, preſerving the old forms; but in the
others, there is often no union or coaleſcence of parts, nor
are any of them equal in merit to thoſe Plays more peculiarly and emphatically *Shakeſpeare's own.* The reader
will be pleaſed to think that I do not reckon into the
works of *Shakeſpeare* certain abſurd productions which
his editors have been ſo good as to compliment him
with. I object, and ſtrenuouſly too, even to *The Tam-
ing of the Shrew*; not that it wants merit, but that it
does not bear the peculiar features and ſtamp of
Shakeſpeare.

The rhyming parts of the Hiſtoric plays are all, I
think, of an older date than the times of *Shakeſpeare.*
—There was a Play, I believe, of *the Acts of King John,*
of which the baſtard *Falconbridge* ſeems to have been
the hero and the fool: He appears to have ſpoken altogether in rhyme. *Shakeſpeare* ſhews him to us in the
latter part of the ſecond ſcene in the firſt act of *King
John* in this condition; tho' he afterwards, in the courſe
of the Play, thought fit to adopt him, to give him language and manners, and to make him his own.

branch of it remained in *Shakespeare*'s time, might have been proud of their Dramatic ally, if indeed they could have any fair pretence to claim as such *him* whom *Shakespeare*, perhaps in contempt of Cowardice, wrote *Falstaff*, not *Fastolfe*, the true Historic name of the Gartered Craven.

In the age of Henry IV. a Family crest and arms were authentic proofs of gentility; and this proof, among others, *Shakespeare* has furnished us with : *Falstaff* always carried about him, it seems, *a Seal ring of his Grandfather's worth*, as he says, *forty marks :* The Prince indeed affirms, but not seriously I think, that this ring was *copper*. As to the existence of the *bonds*, which were I suppose the negotiable securities or paper-money of the time, and which he pretended to have lost, I have nothing to say ; but the ring, I believe, was really gold ; tho' probably a little too much alloyed with baser metal. But this is not the point : The *arms* were doubtless genuine ; they were borne by his Grandfather, and are proofs of an antient gentility ; a gentility doubtless, in

former

former periods, connected with wealth and pof-
feſſions, tho' the gold of the family might have
been tranſmuting by degrees, and perhaps, in the
hands of *Falſtaff*, converted into little better than
copper. This obſervation is made on the ſuppoſition of *Falſtaff*'s being conſidered as the head
of the family, which I think however he ought
not to be. It appears rather as if he ought to
be taken in the light of a cadet or younger brother ; which the familiar appellation of *John*,
" the only one (as he ſays) given him by his bro-
" thers and ſiſters," ſeems to indicate. Be this
as it may, we find he is able, in ſpite of diſſipation,
to keep up a certain *ſtate* and *dignity* of appearance ;
retaining no leſs than four, if not five, followers
or men ſervants in his train. He appears alſo
to have had apartments in town, and, by his in-
vitations of *Maſter Gower* to dinner and to ſupper,
a regular table : And one may infer farther from
the Prince's queſtion, on his return from Wales,
to *Bardolph*, " *Is your maſter* here *in London*," that
he had likewiſe a houſe in the country. Slight
proofs

proofs it muſt be confeſſed, yet the inferences are ſo probable, ſo buoyant, in their own nature, that they may well reſt on them. That he did not lodge at the Tavern is clear from the circumſtances of the arreſt. Theſe various occaſions of expence,—ſervants, taverns, houſes, and whores,— neceſſarily imply that *Falſtaff* muſt have had ſome funds which are not brought immediately under our notice. That theſe funds were not however adequate to his ſtyle of living is plain : Perhaps his train may be confidered only as incumbrances, which the pride of family and the habit of former opulence might have brought upon his preſent poverty : I do not mean abſolute poverty, but call it ſo as relative to his expence. To have " *but ſeven groats* " *and two-pence in his purſe* " and a page to bear it, is truly ridiculous ; and it is for that reaſon we become ſo familiar with its contents, " *He* " *can find*" he ſays, " *no remedy for this conſumption* " *of the purſe, borrowing does but linger and linger* " *it out ; but the diſeaſe is incurable.*" It might well be deemed ſo in his courſe of diſſipation : But I

fhall prefently fuggeft one fource at leaft of his
fupply much more conftant and honourable than
that of borrowing. But the condition of *Falftaff*
as to opulence or poverty is not very material
to my purpofe : It is enough if his birth was
diftinguifhed, and his youth noted for gallantry
and accomplifhments. To the firft I have fpoken,
and as for the latter we fhall not be at a lofs when
we remember that " *he was in his youth a page to*
Thomas Mowbray Duke of Norfolk ;" a fituation
at that time fought for by young men of the beft
families and firft fortune. The houfe of every
great noble was at that period a kind of Military
fchool ; and it is probable that *Falftaff* was fingularly adroit at his exercifes : " *He broke Schoggan's*
" *head,*" (fome boifterous fencer I fuppofe)
" *when he was but a crack thus high.*" *Shallow* remembers him *as notedly fkilful at backfword* ; and
he was at that period, according to his own humourous account, "*fcarcely an eagle's talon in the*
" *waift, and could have crept thro' an alderman's thumb*
" *ring.*" Even at the age at which he is exhibited

to

to us, we find him *foundering*, as he calls it, *nine score and odd miles*, with wonderful expedition, to join the army of Prince John of Lancafter; and declaring after the furrender of *Coleville*, that " *had he but a belly of any indifferency he were fimply* " *the moft active fellow in Europe.*" Nor ought we here to pafs over his Knighthood without notice. It was, I grant, intended by the author as a dignity which, like his Courage and his wit, was to be debafed ; his knighthood by low fituations, his Courage by circumftances and imputations of cowardice, and his wit by buffoonery. But how are we to fuppofe this honour was acquired ? By that very Courage, it fhould feem, which we fo obftinately deny him. It was not certainly given him, like a modern City Knighthood, for his wealth or gravity : It was in thefe days a Military honour, and an authentic badge of Military merit.

But *Falftaff* was not only a Military Knight, he poffefs'd an honourable *penfion* into the bargain ; the reward as well as retainer of fervice, and which feems (befides the favours per-

haps of Mrs. *Urſula*) to be the principal and only
ſolid ſupport of his preſent expences.   But let us
refer to the paſſage.   " *A pox of this gout, or a gout*
" *of this pox*; *for one or the other plays the rogue with*
" *my great toe*: *It is no matter if I do halt, I have the*
" *wars for my colour and my penſion ſhall ſeem the more*
" *reaſonable*."   The mention *Falſtaff* here makes
of a penſion, has I believe been generally conſtrued to refer rather to *hope* than *poſſeſſion*, yet I
know not why: For the poſſeſſive MY, *my penſion*
(not *a* penſion) requires a different conſtruction.
Is it that we cannot enjoy a wit, till we have
ſtript him of every worldly advantage, and reduced him below the level of our envy ? It may be
perhaps for this reaſon among others that *Shakeſpeare* has ſo obſcured the better parts of *Falſtaff*
and ſtolen them ſecretly on our feelings, inſtead
of opening them fairly to the notice of our underſtandings.   How careleſly, and thro' what
bye-paths, as it were, of caſual inference is this
fact of a penſion introduced !   And how has he
aſſociated it with misfortune and infirmity ! Yet
I queſtion

I queſtion, however, if, in this one place the *Impreſſion* which was intended, be well and effectually made. It muſt be left to the reader to determine if in that maſs of things out of which *Falſtaff* is compounded, he ever conſidered a penſion as any part of the compoſition : A penſion however he appears to have had, one that halting could only ſeem to make more reaſonable, not more honourable. The inference ariſing from the fact, I ſhall leave to the reader. It is ſurely a circumſtance highly advantageous to *Falſtaff*, (I ſpeak of the penſions of former days) whether he be conſidered in the light of a ſoldier or a gentleman.

I cannot foreſee the temper of the reader, nor whether he be content to go along with me in theſe kind of obſervations. Some of the incidents which I have drawn out of the Play may appear too minute, whilſt yet they refer to principles, which may ſeem too general. Many points require explanation; ſomething ſhould be ſaid of the nature of *Shakeſpeare's* Dramatic characters;

racters; * by what arts they were formed, and wherein they differ from thofe of other writers; fomething likewife more profeffedly of *Shake-speare*

* The reader muft be fenfible of fomething in the compofition of *Shakefpeare*'s chaiacters, which renders them effentially different from thofe drawn by other writers. The characters of every Drama muft indeed be grouped; but in the groupes of other poets the parts which are not feen, do not in fact exift. But there is a certain roundnefs and integrity in the forms of *Shakefpeare*, which give them an independence as well as a relation, infomuch that we often meet with paffages, which tho' perfectly felt, cannot be fufficiently explained in words, without unfolding the whole character of the fpeaker: And this I may be obliged to do in refpect to that of *Lancafter*, in order to account for fome words fpoken by him in cenfure of *Falftaff.*—Something which may be thought too heavy for the *text*, I fhall add *here*, as a conjecture concerning the compofition of *Shakefpeare*'s characters : Not that they were the effect, I believe, fo much of a minute and laborious attention, as of a certain comprehenfive energy of mind, involving within itfelf all the effects of fyftem and of labour.

ſpeare himſelf, and of the peculiar character of his genius. After ſuch a review we may not perhaps think any conſideration ariſing out of the

Bodies of all kinds, whether of metals, plants, or animals, are ſuppoſed to poſſeſs certain firſt principles of *being*, and to have an exiſtence independent of the accidents, which form their magnitude or growth: Thoſe accidents are ſuppoſed to be drawn in from the ſurrounding elements, but not indiſcriminately; each plant and each animal, imbibes thoſe things only, which are proper to its own diſtinct nature, and which have beſides ſuch a ſecret relation to each other as to be capable of forming a perfect union and coaleſcence: But ſo variouſly are the ſurrounding elements mingled and diſpoſed, that each particular body, even of thoſe under the ſame ſpecies, has yet ſome *peculiar* of its own. *Shakeſpeare* appears to have conſidered the being and growth of the human mind as analogous to this ſyſtem: There are certain qualities and capacities, which he ſeems to have conſidered as firſt principles, the chief of which are certain energies of courage and activity, according to their degrees; together with different degrees and ſorts of ſenſibilities, and a capacity, varying likewiſe in the *degree*, of diſcernment and intelligence. The reſt of the compoſition

the Play, or out of general nature, either as too minute or too extenſive.

Shakeſpeare is in truth, an author whoſe mimic creation agrees in general ſo perfectly with that

of

tion is drawn in from an atmoſphere of ſurrounding things; that is, from the various influences of the different laws, religions and governments in the world; and from thoſe of the different ranks and inequalities in ſociety; and from the different profeſſions of men, encouraging or repreſſing paſſions of particular ſorts, and inducing different modes of thinking and habits of life; and he ſeems to have known intuitively what thoſe influences in particular were which this or that original conſtitution would moſt freely imbibe, and which would moſt eaſily aſſociate and coaleſce. But all theſe things being, in different ſituations, very differently diſpoſed, and thoſe differences exactly diſcerned by him, he found no difficulty in marking every individual, even among characters of the ſame ſort, with ſomething peculiar and diſtinct.—Climate and complexion demand their influence, " *Be thus when thou art dead, and I will kill thee, and love thee after,*" is a ſentiment characteriſtic of, and fit only to be uttered by a *Moor.*

But

of nature, that it is not only wonderful in the
great, but opens another fcene of amazement to the
difcoveries of the microfcope. We have been charged indeed by a Foreign writer with an overmuch
admiring of this *Barbarian*: Whether we have
admired

But it was not enough for *Shakefpeare* to have formed
his characters with the moft perfect truth and coherence; it was further neceffary that he fhould poffefs
a wonderful facility of compreffing, as it were, his
own fpirit into thefe images, and of giving alternate
animation to the forms. This was not to be done
from without, he muft have *felt* every varied fituation, and have fpoken thro' the organ he had formed. Such an intuitive comprehenfion of things and
fuch a facility, muft unite to produce a *Shakefpeare*.
The reader will not now be furprifed if I affirm that
thofe characters in *Shakefpeare*, which are feen only in
part, are yet capable of being unfolded and underftood
in the whole; every part being in fact relative, and
inferring all the reft. It is true that the point of action
or fentiment, which we are moft concerned in, is always held out for our fpecial notice. But who does
not perceive that there is a peculiarity about it, which
conveys a relifh of the whole? And very frequently,
when

admired with knowledge, or have blindly followed thofe feelings of affection which we could
not refift, I cannot tell; but certain it is, that to
the labours of his Editors he has not been overmuch obliged. They are however for the moft
part of the firft rank in literary fame; but fome
of

when no particular point preffes, he boldly makes a
character act and fpeak from thofe parts of the compofition, which are *inferred* only, and not diftinctly
fhewn. This produces a wonderful effect; it feems
to carry us beyond the poet to nature itfelf, and gives
an integrity and truth to facts and character, which
they could not otherwife obtain: And this is in reality that art in *Shakefpeare*, which being withdrawn
from our notice, we more emphatically call *nature*.
A felt propriety and truth from caufes unfeen, I take
to be the higheft point of Poetic compofition. If the
characters of *Shakefpeare* are thus *whole*, and as it were
original, while thofe of almoft all other writers are
mere imitation, it may be fit to confider them rather
as Hiftoric than Dramatic beings, and, when occafion
requires, to account for their conduct from the *whole*
of character, from general principles, from latent motives, and from policies not avowed.

of them had poſſeſſions of their own in Parnaſ-
ſus, of an extent too great and important to allow of a very diligent attention to the intereſts
of others; and among thoſe Critics more
profeſſionally ſo, the ableſt and the beſt has unfortunately looked more to the praiſe of ingenious than of juſt conjecture. The character of
his emendations are not ſo much that of *right*
or *wrong*, as that, being in the extreme, they
are always *Warburtonian*. Another has ſince
undertaken the cuſtody of our author, whom he
ſeems to conſider as a ſort of wild Proteus or madman, and accordingly knocks him down with the
butt-end of his critical ſtaff, as often as he ex-
ceeds that line of ſober diſcretion, which this
learned Editor appears to have chalked out for
him : Yet is this Editor notwithſtanding " a man
take him for all in all," very highly reſpec-
table for his genius and his learning. What
however may be chiefly complained of in theſe
gentlemen is, that having erected themſelves
into the condition, as it were, of guardians and

truſtees

truftees of *Shakefpeare*, they have never undertaken to difcharge the difgraceful incumbrances of fome wretched productions, which have
long hung heavy on his fame. Befides the evidence of tafte, which indeed is not communica-
ble, there are yet other and more general
proofs that thefe incumbrances were not incurred by *Shakefpeare*: The *Latin* fentences difper-
fed thro' the imputed trafh is, I think, of itfelf
a decifive one. *Love's Labour loft* contains a
very conclufive one of another kind; tho' the
very laft Editor has, I believe, in his critical
fagacity, fuppreffed the evidence, and withdrawn
the record.

Yet whatever may be the neglect of fome, or
the cenfure of others, there are thofe, who firmly
believe that this wild, this uncultivated Barbarian, has not yet obtained one half of his fame;
and who truft that fome new Stagyrite will arife,
who inftead of pecking at the furface of things
will enter into the inward foul of his compofitions, and expel by the force of congenial
feelings

feelings, thofe foreign impurities which have ftained and difgraced his page. And as to thofe *fpots* which will ftill remain, they may perhaps become invifible to thofe who fhall feek them thro' the medium of his beauties, inftead of looking for thofe beauties, as is too frequently done, thro' the fmoke of fome real or imputed obfcurity. When the hand of time fhall have brufhed off his prefent Editors and Commentators, and when the very name of *Voltaire*, and even the memory of the language in which he has written, fhall be no more, the *Apalachian* mountains, the banks of the *Ohio*, and the plains of *Sciota* fhall refound with the accents of this Barbarian : In his native tongue he fhall roll the genuine paffions of nature ; nor fhall the griefs of *Lear* be alleviated, or the charms and wit of *Rofalind* be abated by time. There is indeed nothing perifhable about him, except that very learning which he is faid fo much to want. He had not, it is true, enough for the demands of the age in which he lived, but he had perhaps too much for the reach

F

of

of his genius, and the intereſt of his fame. *Milton* and he will carry the decayed remnants and fripperies of antient mythology into more diſtant ages than they are by their own force intitled to extend ; and the metamorphoſes of *Ovid*, upheld by them, lay in a new claim to unmerited immortality.

Shakeſpeare is a name ſo intereſting, that it is excuſable to ſtop a moment, nay it would be indecent to paſs him without the tribute of ſome admiration. He differs eſſentially from all other writers : Him we may profeſs rather to feel than to underſtand ; and it is ſafer to ſay, on many occaſions, that we are poſſeſſed by him, than that we poſſeſs him. And no wonder ;— He ſcatters the ſeeds of things, the principles of character and action, with ſo cunning a hand yet with ſo careleſs an air, and, maſter of our feelings, ſubmits himſelf ſo little to our judgment, that every thing ſeems ſuperior. We diſcern not his courſe, we ſee no connection of cauſe and ef-

fect,

fect, we are rapt in ignorant admiration, and claim no kindred with his abilities. All the incidents, all the parts, look like chance, whilft we feel and are fenfible that the whole is defign. His Characters not only act and fpeak in ftrict conformity to nature, but in ftrict relation to us ; juft fo much is fhewn as is requifite, juft fo much is impreffed ; he commands every paffage to our heads and to our hearts, and moulds us as he pleafes, and that with fo much eafe, that he never betrays his own exertions. We fee thefe Characters act from the mingled motives of paffion, reafon, intereft, habit and complection, in all their proportions, when they are fuppofed to know it not themfelves ; and we are made to acknowledge that their actions and fentiments are, from thofe motives, the neceffary refult. He at once blends and diftinguifhes every thing ;— every thing is complicated, every thing is plain. I reftrain the further expreffions of my admiration left they fhould not feem applicable

to

to man; but it is really aftonifhing that a mere human being, a part of humanity only, fhould fo perfectly comprehend the whole; and that he fhould poffefs fuch exquifite art, that whilft every woman and every child fhall feel the whole effect, his learned Editors and Commentators fhould yet fo very frequently miftake or feem ignorant of the caufe. A fceptre or a ftraw are in his hands of equal efficacy; he needs no felection; he converts every thing into excellence; nothing is too great, nothing is too bafe. Is a character efficient like *Richard*, it is every thing we can wifh: Is it otherwife, like *Hamlet*, it is productive of equal admiration: Action produces one mode of excellence and inaction another: The Chronicle, the Novel, or the Ballad; the king, or the beggar, the hero, the madman, the fot or the fool; it is all one;—nothing is worfe, nothing is better: The fame genius pervades and is equally admirable in all. Or, is a character to be fhewn in progreffive change, and the events

of

of years comprized within the hour ;—with what a Magic hand does he prepare and fcatter his fpells! The Underftanding muft, in the firft place, be fubdued ; and lo! how the rooted prejudices of the child fpring up to confound the man! The Weird fifters rife, and order is extinguifhed. The laws of nature give way, and leave nothing in our minds but wildnefs and horror. No paufe is allowed us for reflection : Horrid fentiment, furious guilt and compunction, air-drawn daggers, murders, ghofts, and inchantment, fhake and *poffefs us wholly.* In the mean time the *procefs* is completed. *Macbeth* changes under our eye, *the milk of human kindnefs is converted to gall* ; *he has fupped full of horrors,* and his *May of life is fallen into the fear, the yellow leaf* ; whilft we, the fools of amazement, are infenfible to the fhifting of place and the lapfe of time, and till the curtain drops, never once wake to the truth of things, or recognize the laws of exiftence.— On fuch an occafion, a fellow, like *Rymer,*

waking from his trance, fhall lift up his Con-
ftable's ftaff, and charge this great Magician,
this daring *practicer of arts inhibited*, in the name
of *Ariftotle*, to furrender ; whilft *Ariftotle* himfelf, difowning his wretched Officer, would
fall proftrate at his feet and acknowledge his
fupremacy.—O fupreme of Dramatic excellence ! (*might he fay,*) not to me be imputed the
infolence of fools. The bards of *Greece* were
confined within the narrow circle of the Chorus,
and hence they found themfelves conftrained to
practice, for the moft part, the precifion, and
copy the details of nature. I followed them,
and knew not that a larger circle might be
drawn, and the Drama extended to the whole
reach of human genius. Convinced, I fee that
a more compendious *nature* may be obtained ;
a nature of *effects* only, to which neither the
relations of place, or continuity of time, are always effential. Nature, condefcending to the
faculties and apprehenfions of man, has drawn
through

through human life a regular chain of viſible cauſes and effects: But Poetry delights in ſurprize, conceals her ſteps, ſeizes at once upon the heart, and obtains the Sublime of things without betraying the rounds of her aſcent: True Poeſy is *magic*, not *nature*; an effect from cauſes hidden or unknown. To the Magician I preſcribed no laws; his law and his power are one; his power is his law. Him, who neither imitates, nor is within the reach of imitation, no precedent can or ought to bind, no limits to contain. If his end is obtained, who ſhall queſtion his courſe? Means, whether apparent or hidden, are juſtified in Poeſy by ſuccefs; but then moſt perfect and moſt admirable when moſt concealed *.——But

F 4　　　　　　　whither

---

* Theſe obſervations have brought me ſo near to the regions of Poetic *magic*, (uſing the word here in its ſtrict and proper ſenſe, and not looſely as in the *text*) that tho' they lie not directly in my courſe, I yet may

　　　　　　　be

whither am I going! This copious and delightful topic has drawn me far beyond my defign: I haften back to my fubject, and am guarded, for a time at leaft, againft any further temptation to digrefs.

I was

be allowed in this place to point the reader that way. A felt propriety, or truth of art, from an unfeen, tho' fuppofed adequate caufe, we call *nature*. A like feeling of propriety and truth, fuppofed without a caufe, or as feeming to be derived from caufes inadequate, fantaftic, and abfurd,—fuch as wands, circles, incantations, and fo forth,—we call by the general name *magic*, including all the train of fuperftition, witches, ghofts, fairies, and the reft.—*Reafon* is confined to the line of vifible exiftence; our *paffions* and our *fancy* extend far beyond into the *obfcure*; but however lawlefs their operations may feem, the images they fo wildly form have yet a relation to truth, and are the fhadows at leaft, however fantaftic, of *reality*. I am not inveftigating but paffing this fubject, and muft therefore leave behind me much curious fpeculation. Of Perfonifications however we fhould obferve that thofe which are made out of abftract ideas are the creatures of the Underftanding only: Thus, of the

mixed

I was confidering the dignity of *Falſtaff* ſo far as it might ſeem connected with, or productive of military merit, and I have aſſigned him *reputation* at leaſt, if not *fame*, noble connection, birth, attendants, title, and an honourable

mixed modes, virtue, beauty, wiſdom and others,—what are they but very obſcure ideas of *qualities* conſidered as abſtracted from any *ſubject* whatever? The mind cannot ſteadily contemplate ſuch an abſtraction: What then does it do?—Invent or imagine a ſubject in order to ſupport theſe qualities; and hence we get the Nymphs or Goddeſſes of virtue, of beauty, or of wiſdom; the very obſcurity of the ideas being the cauſe of their converſion into ſenſible objects, with preciſion both of feature and of form. But as reaſon has its perſonifications, ſo has *paſſion.*—Every paſſion has its Object, tho' often diſtant and obſcure;—to be brought nearer then, and rendered more diſtinct, it is perſonified: and Fancy fantaſtically decks, or aggravates the *form,* and adds "a local habitation and a name." But paſſion is the *dupe* of its own artifice and *realiſes* the image it had formed. The Grecian theology was mixed of both theſe kinds of perſonification. Of the images produced by paſſion it muſt be obſerved that they are

the

nourable penfion ; every one of them prefump-
tive proofs of Military merit, and motives of
action. What deduction is to be made on
thefe articles, and why they are fo much obfcured may, perhaps, hereafter appear.

I have

the images, for the moft part, not of the paffions
themfelves, but of their remote effects. *Guilt* looks
through the medium, and beholds a devil; *fear*, fpec-
tres of every fort; *hope*, a fmiling cherub; *malice* and
envy fee hags, and witches, and inchanters dire ,
whilft the innocent and the young, behold with fearful delight the tripping fairy, whofe fhadowy form the
moon gilds with its fofteft beams.—Extravagant as
all this appears, it has its laws fo precife that we
are fenfible both of a local and temporary, and of an
univerfal magic , the firft derived from the general nature of the human mind, influenced by particular habits,
inftitutions, and climate ; and the latter from the fame
general nature abftracted from thofe confiderations :
Of the firft fort the *machinery* in *Macbeth* is a very
ftriking inftance ; a machinery, which, however exquifite at the time, has already loft more than half its
force ; and the Gallery now laughs in fome places
where it ought to fhudder :—But the magic of the
Tempeft is lafting and univerfal.

There

I have now gone through the examination of all the perfons of the Drama from whofe mouths any thing can be drawn relative to the Courage of *Falftaff*, excepting the *Prince* and *Poins*, whofe evidence I have begged leave to *referve*,

and

There is befides a fpecies of writing for which we have no term of art, and which holds a middle place between nature and magic ; I mean where fancy either alone, or mingled with reafon, or reafon affuming the appearance of fancy, governs fome real exiftence ; but the whole of this art is pourtrayed in a fingle Play, in the real madnefs of *Lear*, in the affumed wildnefs of *Edgar*, and in the Profeffional *Fantafque* of the *Fool*, all operating to contraft and heighten each other. There is yet another feat in this kind, which *Shakefpeare* has performed ;—he has perfonified *malice* in his *Caliban* ; a character kneaded up of three diftinct natures, the diabolical, the human, and the brute. The reft of his preternatural beings are images of *effects* only, and cannot fubfift but in a furrounding atmofphere of thofe paffions, from which they are derived. *Caliban* is the paffion itfelf, or rather a compound of malice, fervility, and luft, *fubftantiated* ; and therefore beft fhewn in contraft with the lightnefs of

Ariel

and excepting a very fevere cenfure paffed on him by Lord *John* of *Lancafter*, which I fhall prefently confider: But I muft firft obferve, that fetting afide the jefts of the *Prince* and *Poins*, and this cenfure of *Lancafter*, there is not one expreffion

Ariel and the innocence of *Miranda.*—*Witches* are fometimes fubftantial exiftences, fuppofed to be poffeffed by, or allyed to the unfubftantial; but the Witches in *Macbeth* are a grofs fort of fhadows, " bubbles of the earth," as they are finely called by *Banquo.*—*Ghofts* differ from other imaginary beings in this, that they belong to no element, have no fpecific nature or character, and are effects, however harfh the expreffion, fuppofed without a caufe; the reafon of which is that they are not the creation of the poet, but the fervile copies or tranfcripts of popular imagination, connected with fuppofed reality and religion. Should the poet affign the true caufe, and call them the mere painting or *coinage of the brain*, he would difappoint his own end, and deftroy the being he had raifed. Should he affign fictitious caufes, and add a fpecific nature, and a local habitation, it would not be endured; or the effect would be loft by the converfion of one being into another. The approach to reality in this cafe defeats

expreffion uttered by any character in the Drama
that can be conftrued into any impeachment of
Falftaff's Courage ;—an obfervation made before
as refpecting fome of the Witneffes ;—it is
now extended to all: And though this filence
be a negative proof only, it cannot, in my opinion, under the circumftances of the cafe, and
whilft uncontradicted by facts, be too much re-
lied on. If *Falftaff* had been intended for the
character of a *Miles Gloriofus*, his behaviour
ought, and therefore would have been com-
mented upon by others. *Shakefpeare* feldom
trufts to the apprehenfions of his audience ; his
characters interpret for one another continually,
and when we leaft fufpect fuch artful and fecret
management

defeats all the arts and managements of fiction.—The
whole play of the *Tempeft* is of fo high and fuperior a
nature that *Dryden*, who had attempted to imitate in
vain, might well exclaim that

    " —*Shakefpeare*'s *magic* could not copied be,
    " Within that circle none durft walk but He.'

management: The conduct of *Shakefpeare* in this refpect is admirable, and I could point out a thoufand paffages which might put to fhame the advocates of a formal Chorus, and prove that there is as little of neceflity as grace in fo mechanic a contrivance *. But I confine my cenfure of the Chorus to its fuppofed ufe of comment and interpretation only.

Falftaff is, indeed, fo far from appearing to my eye in the light of a *Miles Gloriofus*, that in the beft of my tafte and judgment, he does not difcover, except in confequence of the robbery, the leaft *trait* of fuch a character. All his boafting fpeeches are humour, mere humour, and carefully fpoken to perfons who cannot mifapprehend them, who cannot be impofed on: They contain indeed, for the moft part, an unreafonable and imprudent ridicule

of

* Ænobarbus, in Anthony and Cleopatra, is in effect the Chorus of the Play; as Menenius Agrippa is of Coriolanus.

of himfelf, the ufual fubject of his good hu-
moured merriment; but in the company of ignorant people, fuch as the Juftices, or his own
followers, he is remarkably referved, and does
not hazard any thing, even in the way of humour, that may be fubject to miftake : Indeed
he no where feems to fufpect that his character
is open to cenfure on this fide, or that he
needs the arts of impofition.—" *Turk Gregory*
" *never did fuch deeds in arms as I have done this*
" *day,*" is fpoken, whilft he breathes from action,
to the Prince in a tone of jolly humour, and
contains nothing but a light ridicule of his
own inactivity : This is as far from real boafting as his faying before the battle, " *Wou'd it*
" *were bed-time,* Hal, *and all were well,*" is from
meannefs or depreffion. This articulated wifh
is not the fearful outcry of a *Coward,* but the
frank and honeft breathing of a *generous fellow,*
who does not expect to be ferioufly reproached
with the character. Inftead indeed, of deferv-
ing the name of a vain glorious *Coward,* his

modefly

modefty perhaps on this head, and whimfical ridicule of himfelf, have been a principal fource of the imputation.

But to come to the very ferious reproach thrown upon him by that *cold blooded* boy, as he calls him, *Lancafter.*—*Lancafter* makes a folemn treaty of peace with the *Archbifhop of York*, *Mowbray*, &c. upon the faith of which they difperfe their troops ; which is no fooner done than *Lancafter* arrefts the Principals, and purfues the *fcattered ftray :* A tranfaction, by the bye, fo fingularly perfidious, that I wifh *Shakefpeare*, for his own credit, had not fuffered it to pafs under his pen without marking it with the blackeft ftrokes of Infamy.—During this tranfaction, *Falftaff* arrives, joins in the purfuit, and takes Sir *John Coleville* prifoner. Upon being feen by *Lancafter* he is thus addreffed :—

" *Now*

" *Now Falstaff, where have you been all this while ?*
" *When every thing is over then you come :*
" *These tardy tricks of yours will, on my life,*
" *One time or other break some gallows' back.*"

This may appear to many a very formidable passage. It is spoken, as we may say, in the hearing of the army, and by one intitled as it were by his station to decide on military conduct ; and if no punishment immediately follows, the forbearance may be imputed to a regard for the Prince of Wales, whose favour the delinquent was known so unworthily to possess. But this reasoning will by no means apply to the real circumstances of the case. The effect of this passage will depend on the credit we shall be inclined to give to *Lancaster* for integrity and candour, and still more upon the facts which are the ground of this censure, and which are fairly offered by *Shakespeare* to our notice.

G

We

We will examine the evidence arifing from both; and to this end we muft in the firft place a little unfold the character of this young Commander in chief;—from a review of which we may more clearly difcern the general impulfes and fecret motives of his conduct: And this is a proceeding which I think the peculiar character of *Shakefpeare*'s Drama will very well juftify.

We are already well prepared what to think of this young man:—We have juft feen a very pretty manœuvre of his in a matter of the higheft moment, and have therefore the lefs reafon to be furprized if we find him practifing a more petty fraud with fuitable fkill and addrefs. He appears in truth to have been what *Falftaff* calls him, *a cold referved fober-blooded boy*; a politician, as it fhould feem, by nature; bred up moreover in the fchool of *Bolingbroke* his father, and tutored to betray: With fufficient courage and ability perhaps, but with too much of the

knave

knave in his compofition, and too little of enthufiafm, ever to be a great and fuperior character. That fuch a youth as this fhould, even from the propenfities of character alone, take any plaufible occafion to injure a frank unguarded man of wit and pleafure, will not appear unnatural. But he had other inducements. *Falftaff* had given very general fcandal by his diftinguifhed wit and noted poverty, infomuch that a little cruelty and injuftice towards him was likely to pafs, in the eye of the grave and prudent part of mankind, as a very creditable piece of fraud, and to be accounted to *Lancafter* for virtue and good fervice. But *Lancafter* had motives yet more prevailing ; *Falftaff* was a Favourite, without the power which belongs to that character ; and the tone of the Court was ftrongly againft him, as the mifleader and corrupter of the Prince ; who was now at too great a diftance to afford him immediate countenance and protection. A fcratch then, between jeft and earneft as it

G 2

were,

were, fomething that would not too much offend the prince, yet would leave behind a difgraceful fcar upon *Falſtaff*, was very fuitable
to the temper and fituation of parties and affairs. With thefe obfervations in our thought
let us return to the paffage : It is plainly intended for difgrace, but how artful, how cautious, how infidious is the manner ! It may
pafs for fheer pleafantry and humour : *Lancaſter*
affumes the familiar phrafe and *girding* tone
of *Harry*; and the gallows, as he words it,
appears to be in the moſt danger from an encounter with *Falſtaff*.—With refpeᴄt to the matter, 'tis a kind of *miching malicho* ; it means
mifchief indeed, but there is not precifion enough
in it to intitle it to the appellation of a formal
charge, or to give to *Falſtaff* any certain and
determined ground of defence. *Tardy tricks* may
mean, not Cowardice but negleᴄt only, though
the *manner* may feem to carry the imputation to both.—The reply of *Falſtaff* is exaᴄtly
fuited to the qualities of the fpeech ;—for

Falſtaff

Falftaff never wants ability but conduct only.
He anfwers the general effect of this fpeech,
by a feeling and ferious complaint of injuftice ; he then goes on to apply his defence to
the vindication both of his diligence and courage ; but he deferts by degrees his ferious tone,
and taking the handle of pleafantry which
Lancafter had held forth to him, he is pru-
dently content, as being fenfible of *Lancafter*'s
high rank and ftation, to let the whole pafs off
in buffoonery and humour. But the queftion
is, however, not concerning the adroitnefs and
management of either party : Our bufinefs is,
after putting the credit of *Lancafter* out of the
queftion, to difcover what there may be of truth
and of fact either in the charge of the one, or
the defence of the other. From this only,
we fhall be able to draw our inferences with
fairnefs and with candour. The charge againft
Falftaff is already in the poffeffion of the reader : The defence follows.—

Falf. "*I would be forry, my lord, but it fhould*
"*be thus : I never knew yet but that rebuke and*
"*check were the reward of valour.* *Do you think*
"*me a fwallow, an arrow, or a bullet?* *Have I*
"*in my poor and old motion the expedition of*
"*thought?* *I fpeeded hither within the very ex-*
"*tremeft inch of poffibility.* *I have foundered nine-*
"*fcore and odd pofts,* (deferting by degrees his
"ferious tone, for *one* of more addrefs and ad-
"vantage) *and here travel-tainted as I am, have I*
"*in my pure and immaculate valour taken Sir John*
"*Coleville of the dale, a moft furious Knight and*
"*valorous enemy.*"

Falftaff's anfwer then is, that he ufed all poffible expedition to join the army; the not
doing of which, with an implication of Cowardice as the caufe, is the utmoft extent of
the charge againft him; and to take off this
implication he refers to the evidence of a fact
prefent and manifeft,—the furrender of *Coleville*;
in whofe hearing he fpeaks, and to whom
therefore

therefore he is fuppofed to appeal. Nothing then remains but that we fhould inquire if *Falftaff*'s anfwer was really founded in truth ; " *I fpeeded hither,* fays he, *within the extremeft inch* " *of poffibility :*" If it be fo, he is juftified : But I am afraid, for we muft not conceal any thing, that *Falftaff* was really detained too long by his debaucheries in London ; at leaft, if we take the Chief Juftice's words very ftrictly.

" Ch. Juft. *How now, Sir John ? What are you* " *brawling here ? Doth this become your* PLACE, *your* " TIME, *your* BUSINESS ? *You fhould have been well* " *on your way to York.*"

Here then feems to be a delay worthy perhaps of rebuke ; and if we could fuppofe *Lancafter* to mean nothing more by *tardy tricks* than idlenefs and debauch, I fhould not poffibly think myfelf much concerned to vindicate *Falftaff* from the charge ; but the words imply, to my apprehenfion, a defigned and deliberate

H 2   G 4   avoidance

avoidance of danger. Yet to the contrary of this we are furnished with very full and complete evidence. *Falstaff*, the moment he quits London, difcovers the utmoft eagernefs and impatience to join the army; he gives up his gluttony, his mirth, and his eafe. We fee him take up in his paffage fome recruits at *Shallow*'s houfe; and tho' he has pecuniary views upon *Shallow*, no inducement ftops him; he takes no refrefhment, he cannot *tarry dinner*, he hurries off; "*I will not*, fays he to the Juftices, "*ufe many words with you. Fare ye well Gentle-* "*men both; I thank ye, I muft a dozen miles to* *night.*"— He mifufes, it is true, at this time the *King's Prefs damnably*; but that does not concern me, at leaft not for the prefent; it belongs to other parts of his character.—It appears then manifeftly that *Shakefpeare* meant to fhew *Falstaff* as really ufing the utmoft fpeed in his power; he arrives almoft literally *within the* *extremeft inch of poffibility*; and if *Lancafter* had not accelerated the event by a ftroke of perfidy

much

much more fubject to the imputation of
Cowardice than the *Debauch* of *Falſtaff*, he
would have been time enough to have ſhared
in the danger of a fair and honeſt deciſion.
But great men have it ſeems a priviledge ;
" *that in the* General's *but a choleric word,*
" *which in the* Soldier *were flat blaſphemy.*"
Yet after all, *Falſtaff* did really come time
enough, as it appears, to join in the villain-
ous triumphs of the day, to take priſoner
*Coleville of the dale, a moſt furious Knight and
valorous enemy.*—Let us look to the fact.
If this incident ſhould be found to contain
any ſtriking proof of *Falſtaff*'s Courage and
Military fame, his defence againſt *Lancaſter*
will be ſtronger than the reader has even a
right to demand. *Falſtaff* encounters *Coleville* in
the field, and having demanded his name,
is ready to aſſail him ; but *Coleville* aſks him
if he is not Sir *John Falſtaff* ; thereby implying
a purpoſe of ſurrender. *Falſtaff* will not ſo much
as furniſh him with a pretence, and anſwers
only,

only, that *he is as good a man.* " *Do you yield Sir,*
or shall I sweat for you ? " *I think,* says Coleville
" *you are Sir John Falstaff, and in that thought*
" *yield me.*" This fact, and the incidents
with which it is accompanied, speak loudly;
it seems to have been contrived by the author on purpose to take off a rebuke so autho-
ritatively made by *Lancaster.* The fact is set
before our eyes to confute the censure : *Lan-*
caster himself seems to give up his charge,
tho' not his ill will ; for upon *Falstaff*'s asking
leave to pass through Glostershire, and artfully desiring that, upon *Lancaster*'s return to
Court, *he might stand well in his report,* *Lan-*
caster seems in his answer to mingle malice
and acquital. " *Fare ye well,* Falstaff, *I in my*
" *condition shall better speak of you than you*
deserve. I would, says Falstaff, who is left
behind in the scene, " *You had but the*
" *wit ; 'twere better than your Dukedom.*" He
continues on the stage some time chewing the
cud of dishonour, which, with all his facility,
he

he cannot well fwallow. " *Good faith* " fays he, accounting to himfelf as well as he could for the injurious conduct of *Lancafter*; " *this* " *fober-blooded boy does not love me.*" This he might well believe. " *A man,* fays he, *cannot* " *make him laugh; there's none of thefe demure* " *boys come to any proof; but that's no marvel,* " *they drink no fack.*"—*Falftaff* then it feems knew no drinker of fack who was a Coward ; at leaft the inftance was not home and fami- liar to him.—" *They all,* fays he, *fall into a kind* " *of Male green ficknefs, and are generally fools and* " *Cowards.*" Anger has a privilege, and I think *Falftaff* has a right to turn the tables upon *Lancafter* if he can ; but *Lancafter* was certainly no fool, and I think upon the whole, no Cow- ard ; yet the Male green ficknefs which *Fal- ftaff* talks of, feems to have infected his man- ners and afpect, and taken from him all external indication of gallantry and courage. He behaves in the battle of Shrewfbury beyond the promife of his complexion and deportment :

" *By*

" *By heaven thou haft deceived me Lancaster*, fays Harry, " *I did not think thee Lord of fuch a fpirit !* Nor was his father lefs furprized " *at his holding Lord Percy at the point with luftier maintenance than he did look for from fuch an unripe warrior.*" But how well and unexpectedly foever he might have behaved upon that occafion, he does not feem to have been of a temper to truft fortune too much or too often with his fafety ; therefore it is that, in order to keep the event in his own hands, he loads the Die, in the prefent cafe, with villainy and deceit : The event however he pioufly afcribes, like a wife and prudent youth as he is, without paying that worfhip to himfelf which he fo juftly merits, to the fpecial favour and interpofition of Heaven.

" *Strike up your drums, purfue the fcattered ftray.*
" *Heaven, and not we, have fafely fought to-day.*"

But the prophane *Falftaff*, on the contrary, lefs informed and lefs ftudious of fupernatural

things,

things, imputes the whole of this conduct to thin potations, and the not drinking largely of good and excellent *sherris*; and so little doubt does he seem to entertain of the Cowardice and ill disposition of this youth, that he stands devising causes, and casting about for an hypothesis on which the whole may be physically explained and accounted for ;—but I shall leave him and Doctor *Cadogan* to settle that point as they may.

The only serious charge against *Falstaff*'s Courage, we have now at large examined ; it came from great authority, from the Commander in chief, and was meant as chastifement and rebuke ; but it appears to have been founded in ill-will, in the particular character of *Lancaster*, and in the wantonness and insolence of power ; and the author has placed near, and under our notice, full and ample proofs of its injustice.—And thus the deeper we look into *Falstaff*'s character, the stronger is our conviction that he was not in-

tended

tended to be fhewn as a Conftitutional coward :
Cenfure cannot lay fufficient hold on him,—and
even malice turns away, and more than half
pronounces his acquittal.

But as yet we have dealt principally in parole
and circumftantial evidence, and have referred
to *Faƌ* only incidentally. But *Faƌs* have a
much more operative influence : They may
be produced, not as arguments only, but Records; not to difpute alone, but to decide.—It
is time then to behold *Falftaff* in aƌual fervice
as a foldier, in danger, and in battle. We
have already difplayed one faƌ in his defence
againft the cenfure of *Lancafter*; a faƌ extremely unequivocal and decifive. But the
reader knows I have others, and doubtlefs goes
before me to the aƌion at *Shrewfbury.* In the
midft and in the heat of battle we fee him
come forwards ;—what are his words ? " *I*
" *have led my Rag-o-muffians where they are peppered* ;
" *there's not three of my hundred and fifty left alive.*"

But

But to *whom* does he fay this? To himfelf only; he fpeaks *in foliloquy.* There is no queftioning the fact, *he had* led *them; they were peppered; there were not* three *left alive.* He was in luck, being in bulk equal to any two of them, to efcape unhurt. Let the author anfwer for that, I have nothing to do with it: He was the Poetic maker of the whole *Corps,* and he might difpofe of them as he pleafed. Well might the Chief juftice, as we now find, acknowledge *Falftaff*'s fervices in this day's battle; an acknowledgment, which amply confirms the fact. A Modern officer, who had performed a feat of this kind, would expect, not only the praife of having done his duty, but the appellation of a hero. But poor *Falftaff* has too much wit to thrive: In fpite of probability, in fpite of inference, in fpite of fact, he muft be a Coward ftill. He happens unfortunately to have more Wit than Courage, and therefore we are malicioufly determined that he fhall have no Courage at all. But let us fuppofe that his modes of expref-

fion

(96)

fion, even *in foliloquy*, will admit of fome abatement ;—how much fhall we abate ? Say that he brought off *fifty* inftead of *three* ; yet a Modern captain would be apt to look big after an action with two thirds of his men, as it were, in his belly. Surely *Shakefpeare* never meant to exhibit this man as a Conftitutional coward ; if he did, his means were fadly deftructive of his end. We fee him, after he had expended his Rag-o-muffians, with fword and target in the midft of battle, in perfect poffeffion of himfelf, and replete with humour and jocularity. He was, I prefume, in fome immediate perfonal danger, in danger alfo of a general defeat ; too corpulent for flight ; and to be led a prifoner was probably to be led to execution ; yet we fee him laughing and eafy, offering a bottle of fack to the Prince inftead of a piftol, punning, and telling him, " *there was that which would* fack *a* " *city.*"—" *What is it a time,* (fays the Prince) " *to jeft and dally now ?* " No, a fober character

would

would not jeſt on ſuch an occaſion, but a Coward could not; he would neither have the inclination, or the power. And what could ſupport *Falſtaff* in ſuch a ſituation? Not principle; he is not ſuſpected of the Point of honour; he ſeems indeed fairly to renounce it. "*Ho-*
"*nour cannot ſet a leg or an arm; it has no ſkill in*
"*ſurgery :—What is it? a word only; meer air. It*
"*is inſenſible to the dead; and detraction will not*
"*let it live with the living.*" What then, but a ſtrong natural conſtitutional Courage, which nothing could extinguiſh or diſmay?—In the following paſſages the true character of *Falſtaff* as to Courage and Principle is finely touched, and the different colours at once nicely blended and diſtinguiſhed. "*If Percy be alive, I'll* pierce
"*him. If he do come in my way, ſo :—If he*
"*do not, if I come in* his *willingly, let him make a*
"*Carbonado of me. I like not ſuch grinning honour*
"*as Sir Walter hath; give me life; which, if I can*
"*ſave, ſo; if not, honour comes unlook'd for, and*
"*there's an end.*" One cannot ſay which pre-

vails

vails moſt here, profligacy or courage; they
are both tinged alike by the ſame humour,
and mingled in one common maſs; yet when
we conſider the ſuperior force of *Percy*, as we
muſt preſently alſo that of *Douglas*, we ſhall
be apt, I believe, in our ſecret heart, to forgive him. Theſe paſſages are ſpoken in ſoliloquy and in battle: If every ſoliloquy made
under ſimilar circumſtances were as audible
as *Falſtaff*'s, the imputation might perhaps
be found too general for cenſure. Theſe
are among the paſſages that have impreſſed
on the world an idea of Cowardice in
Falſtaff;—yet why? He is reſolute to take
his fate: If *Percy* do come in his way, *ſo*;—
if not, he will not ſeek inevitable deſtruction;
he is willing to ſave his life, but if that cannot be, why,—"honour comes unlook'd for,
and there's an end." This ſurely is not the
language of Cowardice: It contains neither
the Bounce or Whine of the character; he de-
rides, it is true, and ſeems to renounce that
grinning idol of Military zealots, *Honour*. But

Falſtaff

Falſtaff was a kind of Military free-thinker, and has accordingly incurred the obloquy of his condition. He ſtands upon the ground of natural Courage only and common ſenſe, and has, it ſeems, too much wit for a hero.—But let me be well underſtood;—I do not juſtify *Falſtaff* for renouncing the point of honour; it proceeded doubtleſs from a general relaxation of mind, and profligacy of temper. Honour is calculated to aid and ſtrengthen natural courage, and lift it up to heroiſm; but natural courage, which can act as ſuch without honour, is natural courage ſtill; the very quality I wiſh to maintain to *Falſtaff*. And if, without the aid of honour, he can act with firmneſs, his portion is only the more eminent and diſtinguiſhed. In ſuch a character, it is to his actions, not his ſentiments, that we are to look for conviction. But it may be ſtill further urged in behalf of *Falſtaff*, that there may be falſe honour as well as falſe religion. It is true; yet even in that caſe, candour obliges

me

me to confefs, that the beft men are moft
difpofed to conform, and moft likely to become the dupes of their own virtue. But it
may however be more reafonably urged, that
there are particular tenets both in honour and
religion, which it is the grofsnefs of folly
not to queftion. To feek out, to court affured
deftruction, without leaving a fingle benefit
behind, may be well reckoned in the number:
And this is precifely the very folly which
Falftaff feems to abjure;—nor are we, perhaps
intitled to fay more, in the way of cenfure,
than that he had not virtue enough to become the dupe of honour, nor prudence
enough to hold his tongue. I am willing however, if the reader pleafes, to compound this
matter, and acknowledge, on my part, that
Falftaff was in all refpects the *old foldier*;
that he had put himfelf under the fober dif-
cipline of difcretion, and renounced, in a great
degree at leaft, what he might call, the Vanities and Superftitions of honour; if the reader

will

will, on his part, admit that this might well be, without his renouncing, at the fame time, the natural firmnefs and refolution he was born to.

But there is a formidable objection behind. *Falftaff* counterfeits bafely on being attacked by *Douglas*; he affumes, in a cowardly fpirit, the appearance of death to avoid the reality. But there was no equality of force; not the leaft chance for victory, or life. And is it the duty then, *think we ftill*, of true Courage, to meet, without benefit to fociety, *certain death ?* Or is it only the phantafy of honour ?—But fuch a fiction is highly difgraceful;—true, and a man of nice honour might perhaps have *grinned* for it. But we muft remember that *Falftaff* had a double character; he was a *wit* as well as a *foldier*; and his Courage, however eminent, was but the *acceffary*; his wit was the *principal*; and the part, which, if they fhould come in competition, he had the greateſt intereſt in maintaining. Vain indeed were the licentiouſneſs of his principles, if he ſhould ſeek death like a bigot, yet without the meed of honour; when he might live by wit, and encreaſe the reputation of that wit by living. But why do I labour this point? It has been already anticipated, and our improved acquaintance with *Falſtaff* will now require no more than a ſhort narrative of the faét.

Whilſt in the battle of Shrewſbury he is exhorting and encouraging the Prince who is engaged with the *Spirit Percy*—"*Well ſaid Hal, to him Hal,*"—he is himſelf attacked by the *Fiend Douglas.* There was no match; nothing remained but death or ſtratagem; grinning honour, or laughing life. But an expedient offers, a mirthful one,—Take your choice *Falſtaff*, a point of honour, or a point of drollery.—It could not be a queſtion;—*Falſtaff* falls, *Douglas* is cheated, and the world laughs. But does he fall like a Coward?
No

No, like a buffoon only; the superior principle prevails, and *Falstaff* lives by a stratagem growing out of his character, to prove himself *no counterfeit*, to jest, to be employed, and to fight again. That *Falstaff* valued himself, and expected to be valued by others, upon this piece of saving wit is plain. It was a stratagem, it is true; it argued presence of mind; but it was moreover, what he most liked, a very laughable joke; and as such he considers it; for he continues to counterfeit after the danger is over, that he may also deceive the Prince, and improve the event into more laughter. He might, for ought that appears, have concealed the transaction; the Prince was too earnestly engaged for observation; he might have formed a thousand excuses for his fall; but he lies still and listens to the pronouncing of his epitaph by the Prince with all the waggish glee and levity of his character. The circumstance of his wounding *Percy* in the thigh, and carrying

I 2

the

the dead body on his back like luggage, is *indecent* but not cowardly. The declaring, though in jeft, that he killed *Percy*, feems to me *idle*, but it is not meant or calculated for *impofition*; it is fpoken to the *Prince himfelf*, the man in the world who could not be, or be fuppofed to be impofed on. But we muft hear, whether to the purpofe or not, what it is that *Harry* has to fay over the remains of his old friend.

> *P. Hen.* What old acquaintance! could not
>   all this flefh
> Keep in a little life? Poor *Jack* farewell!
> I could have better fpared a better man.
> Oh! I fhou'd have a heavy mifs of thee,
> If I were much in love with vanity.
> Death hath not ftruck fo fat a *deer* to-day,
> Tho' many a *dearer* in this bloody fray;
> Imbowelled will I fee thee by and by;
> Till then, in blood by noble *Percy* lye.

This

This is wonderfully proper for the occafion; it is affectionate, it is pathetic, yet it remembers his vanities, and, with a faint gleam of recollected mirth, even his plumpnefs and corpulency; but it is a pleafantry foftned and rendered even vapid by tendernefs, and it goes off in the fickly effort of a miferable pun*.—But to our immediate purpofe,—why is not his Cowardice remembered too? what no furprize that *Falftaff* fhould

---

* The cenfure commonly paffed on *Shakefpeare's puns*, is, I think, not well founded. I remember but very few, which are undoubtedly his, that may not be juftifyed; and if *fo*, a greater inftance cannot be given of the art which he fo peculiarly poffeffed of converting bafe things into excellence.

> " For if the Jew do cut but deep enough,
> " I'll pay the forfeiture *with all my heart.*"

A play upon words is the moft that can be expected from one who affects gaiety under the preffure of fevere misfortunes; but fo imperfect, fo broken a gleam,

can

fhould lye by the fide of the noble *Percy* in the bed of honour ! No reflection that flight, though unfettered by difeafe, could not avail; that fear could not find a fubterfuge from death ? Shall his corpulency and his vanities be recorded, and his more characteriftic quality of Cowardice, even in the moment that it particularly demanded notice and reflection, be forgotten ? If by fparing a better man be here meant a *better foldier*, there is no doubt but there were better Soldiers in the army, more active, more young, more principled, more knowing; but none, it feems, taken for all in all, more acceptable. The comparative *better* ufed here leaves to *Falftaff* the praife at leaft of *good*; and to be a good foldier,

is

can only ferve more plainly to difclofe the gloom and darknefs of the mind; it is an effort of fortitude, which failing in its operation, becomes the trueft, becaufe the moft unaffected *pathos*; and a fkilful actor, well managing his tone and action, might with this miferable pun, fleep a whole audience fuddenly in tears.

is to be a great way from Coward. But *Falftaff*'s goodnefs, in this fort, appears to have been not only enough to redeem him from difgrace, but to mark him with reputation ; if I was to add with *eminence* and *diftinction*, the funeral honours, which are intended for his obfequies, and his being bid, till then, *to lye in blood by the noble Percy*, would fairly bear me out.

Upon the whole of the paffages yet before us, why may I not reafonably hope that the good natured reader, (and I write to no other) not offended at the levity of this exercife, may join with me in thinking that the character of *Falftaff* as to valour, may be fairly and honeftly fummed up in the very words which he himfelf ufes to *Harry* ; and which feem, as to this point, to be intended by *Shakefpeare* as a *Compendium* of his character. " *What*, fays the Prince, *a Coward Sir John Paunch !*" *Falftaff* replies, " *Indeed I* " *am not* John of Gaunt *your grandfather, but yet* " *no Coward, Hal.*"

The

The robbery at *Gadſhill* comes now to be conſidered. But *here*, after ſuch long argumenta-
tion, we may be allowed to breath a little.

I know not what Impreſſion has been made
on the reader; a good deal of evidence has been
produced, and much more remains to be offered.
But how many ſorts of men are there whom
no evidence can perſuade! How many, who
ignorant of *Shakeſpeare*, or forgetful of the text,
may as well read heathen Greek, or the laws
of the land, as this unfortunate Commentary?
How many, who proud and pedantic, hate all
novelty, and damn it without mercy under one
compendious word, Paradox? How many more,
who not deriving their opinions immediately
from the ſovereignty of reaſon, hold at the will
of ſome ſuperior lord, to whom accident or inclination has attached them, and who, true to
their vaſſalage, are reſolute not to ſurrender,
without expreſs permiſſion, their baſe and ill-
gotten poſſeſſions. Theſe, however habited, are

the

the mob of mankind, who hoot and holla, hifs
or huzza, juft as their various leaders may direct. I *challenge* the whole Pannel as not holding by free tenure, and therefore not competent
to the purpofe either of condemnation or acquittal. But to the men of very nice honour what
fhall be faid? I fpeak not of your men of good
fervice, but fuch as Mr. * * * * " *Souls made
of fire*, and *children of the fun*." Thefe gentlemen,
I am fadly afraid, cannot in honour or prudence
admit of any compofition in the very nice article of Courage; *fufpicion* is *difgrace*, and they
cannot ftay to parley with difhonour. The mif-
fortune in cafes of this kind, is, that it is not
eafy to obtain a fair and impartial Jury: When
we cenfure others with an eye to our own ap-
plaufe, we are as feldom fparing of reproach,
as inquifitive into circumftance; and bold is
the man, who tenacious of juftice, fhall venture
to weigh circumftances, or draw lines of diftinction between Cowardice and any apparently fimilar or neighbour quality: As well may a lady,

virgin

virgin or matron, of immaculate honour, prefume to pity or palliate the foft failing of fome
unguarded friend, and thereby confefs, as it were,
thofe fympathetic feelings which it behoves her
to conceal under the moft contemptuous difdain ;
a difdain, always proportioned, I believe, to a
certain confcioufnefs which we muft not explain.
I am afraid that poor *Falftaff* has fuffered not a
little, and may yet fuffer by this faftidioufnefs of
temper. But though we may find thefe claffes
of men rather unfavourable to our wifhes, the
Ladies, one may hope, whofe fmiles are moft
worth our ambition, may be found more pro-
pitious; yet they too, through a generous conformity to the *brave*, are apt to take up the high
tone of honour. Heroifm is an idea perfectly
conformable to the natural delicacy and ele-
vation of their minds. Should we be fortunate
enough therefore to redeem *Falftaff* from the imputations of Cowardice, yet plain Courage, I
am afraid, will not ferve the turn : Even their
heroes, I think, muft be for the moft part in the
bloom

bloom of youth, or *juſt where youth ends, in man-*
hood's freſheſt prime; but to be " *Old, cold, and of*
" *intolerable entrails ; to be fat and greaſy ; as poor*
" *as Job, and as ſlanderous as Satan* ;"—Take him
away, he merits not a fair trial ; he is too of-
fenſive to be turned, too odious to be touched.
I grant, indeed that the ſubjeꞓt of our leꞓture
is not without his infirmity ; " *He cuts three in-*
" *ches on the ribs, he was ſhort-winded,*" and his
breath poſſibly not of the ſweeteſt : " *He had the*
" *gout,*" or ſomething worſe, " *which played the*
" *rogue with his great toe.*"—But theſe conſidera-
tions are not to the point ; we ſhall conceal, as
much as may be, theſe offences ; our buſineſs is
with his *heart* only, which, as we ſhall endeavour
to demonſtrate, lies in the right place, and is
firm and ſound, notwithſtanding a few indica-
tions to the contrary.—As for you, *Mrs.* MON-
TAGUE, I am grieved to find that *you* have been
involved in a Popular error ; ſo much you muſt
allow me to ſay ;—for the reſt, I bow to your
genius and your virtues : You have given to the
world

world a very elegant compofition; and I am
told your manners and your mind are yet more
pure, more elegant than your book. *Falftaff*
was too grofs, too infirm, for your infpection;
but if you durft have looked nearer, you would
not have found Cowardice in the number of
his infirmities.—We will try if we cannot redeem him from this univerfal cenfure.—Let
the venal corporation of authors duck *to the gol-
den fool*, let them fhape their fordid quills to the
mercenary ends of unmerited praife, or of bafer
detraction;—*old Jack* though deferted by princes,
though cenfured by an ungrateful world, and
perfecuted from age to age by Critic and Commentator, and though never rich enough to
hire one literary proftitute, fhall find a Voluntary
defender; and that too at a time when the
whole body of the *Nabobry* demands and requires
defence; whilft their ill-gotten and almoft un-
told gold feels loofe in their unaffured grafp,
and whilft they are ready to fhake off portions of
the enormous heap, that they may the more
fecurely

fecurely clafp the remainder.—But not to digrefs without end,—to the candid, to the
chearful, to the elegant reader we appeal ;
our exercife is much too light for the four eye
of ftrict feverity; it profeffes amufement only,
but we hope of a kind more rational than the
Hiftory of Mifs *Betfy*, eked out with the
Story of Mifs *Lucy*, and the Tale of Mr.
Twankum : And fo, in a leifure hour, and with
the good natured reader, it may be hoped,
to friend, we return, with an air as bufy and
important as if we were engaged in the grave
office of meafuring the *Pyramids*, or fettling
the antiquity of *Stonehenge*, to converfe with
this jovial, this fat, this roguifh, this frail,
but, I think, *not cowardly* companion.

Though the robbery at *Gads-Hill*, and the
fuppofed Cowardice of *Falftaff* on that occafion, are next to be confidered, yet I muft
previoufly declare, that I think the difcuffion
of this matter to be *now* uneffential to the

I   re-eftablifhment

re-eſtabliſhment of *Falſtaff*'s reputation as a man of Courage. For ſuppoſe we ſhould grant, in form, that *Falſtaff* was ſurprized with fear in this ſingle inſtance, that he was off his guard, and even acted like a Coward; what will follow, but that *Falſtaff*, like greater heroes, had his weak moment, and was not exempted from panic and ſurprize? If a ſingle exception can deſtroy a general character, *Hector* was a *Coward*, and *Anthony* a *Poltroon*. But for theſe ſeeming contradictions of Character we ſhall ſeldom be at a loſs to account, if we carefully refer to circumſtance and ſituation.—In the preſent inſtance, *Falſtaff* had done an illegal act; the exertion was over; and he had unbent his mind in ſecurity. The ſpirit of enterprize, and the animating principle of hope, were withdrawn:—In this ſituation, he is unexpectedly attacked; he has no time to recall his thoughts, or bend his mind to action. He is not now acting in the Profeſſion and in the Habits of a

Soldier;

Soldier; he is affociated with known Cowards;
his affailants are vigorous, fudden, and bold;
he is confcious of guilt; he has dangers to
dread of every form, prefent and future; pri-
fons and gibbets, as well as fword and fire;
he is furrounded with darknefs, and the Sheriff,
the Hangman, and the whole *Poffe Commitatus*
may be at his heels :—Without a moment
for reflection, is it wonderful that, under
thefe circumftances, " *he fhould run and roar, and*
" *carry his guts away with as much dexterity as*
" *poffible ?* "

But though I might well reft the queftion
on this ground, yet as there remains many
good topics of vindication; and as I think
a more minute inquiry into this matter will
only bring out more evidence in fupport of
Falftaff's conftitutional Courage, I will not de-
cline the difcuffion. I beg permiffion therefore to ftate fully, as well as fairly, the

I 2   whole

whole of this obnoxious tranfaction, this unfortunate robbery at *Gads-Hill.*

In the fcene wherein we become firft acquainted with *Falftaff*, his character is opened
in a manner worthy of *Shakefpeare* : We fee him
in a green old age, mellow, frank, gay, eafy,
corpulent, loofe, unprincipled, and luxurious ;
a *Robber*, as he fays, *by his vocation* ; yet not
altogether fo :—There was much, it feems, of
mirth and *recreation* in the cafe : " *The poor
abufes of the times,*" he wantonly and humouroufly
tells the Prince "*want countenance* ; *and he hates
to fee refolution fobbed off, as it is, by the rufty
curb of old father antic, the law.*"—When he
quits the fcene, we are acquainted that he is
only paffing to the Tavern : "*Farewell,*" fays
he, with an air of carelefs jollity and gay content, "*You will find me in Eaft-Cheap.*" "*Fare-*
"*well,*" fays the Prince, "*thou latter fpring ;*
"*farewell, all hallown fummer.*" But though all
this is excellent for *Shakefpeare*'s purpofes, we
find

find, as yet at leaft, no hint of *Falftaff*'s Cowardice, no appearance of Braggadocio, or any
preparation whatever for laughter under this
head.—The inftant *Falftaff* is withdrawn, *Poins*
opens to the *Prince* his meditated fcheme of a
double robbery ; and here then we may reafonably expect to be let into thefe parts of
Falftaff's character.—We fhall fee.

Poins. *Now my good fweet lord, ride with us to-*
" *morrow* ; *I have a jeft to execute that I cannot*
" *manage alone.* Falftaff, Bardolph, Peto, *and*
" Gadfhill *fhall rob thofe men that we have already*
" *waylaid* ; *yourfelf and I will not be there* ; *and*
" *when they have the booty, if you and I do not*
" *rob them, cut this head from off my fhoulders.*"

This is giving ftrong furety for his words ;
perhaps he thought the cafe required it : *But*
" *how*, fays the Prince, *fhall we part with them in*
" *fetting forth ?*" *Poins* is ready with his anfwer ;
he had matured the thought, and could folve

every difficulty :—" *They could set out before, or*
" *after ; their horses might be tied in the wood ;*
" *they could change their visors ; and he had al-*
" *ready procured cases of* buckram *to inmask their*
" *outward garments.*" This was going far ; it was
doing business in good earnest. But if we
look into the Play we shall be better able to
account for this activity ; we shall find that
there was, at least as much malice as jest in
Poins's intention. The rival situations of *Poins*
and *Falstaff* had produced on both sides much
jealousy and ill will, which occasionally appears, in *Shakespeare*'s manner, by side lights,
without confounding the main action ; and by
the little we see of this *Poins*, he appears to be
an unamiable, if not a very brutish and bad,
character.—But to pass this ;—the Prince next
says, with a deliberate and wholesome caution,
" *I doubt they will be too hard for us.*" *Poins*'s reply
is remarkable ; " *Well, for* two *of them, I know*
" *them to be as true bred Cowards as ever turned back ;*
" *and for the* third, *if he fights longer than he*
                                                    " *sees*

"*fees caufe, I will forfwear arms.*" There is in
this reply a great deal of management:
There were *four* perfons in all, as *Poins* well
knew, and he had himfelf, but a little before,
named them,—*Falftaff, Bardolph, Peto,* and *Gadfhill*; but now he omits one of the number,
which muft be either *Falftaff*, as not fubject
to any imputation in point of Courage; and
in that cafe *Peto* will be the *third*;—or, as I
rather think, in order to diminifh the force of the
Prince's objection, he artfully drops *Gadfhill*,
who was then out of town, and might therefore be fuppofed to be lefs in the Prince's
notice; and upon this fuppofition *Falftaff* will
be the *third, who will not fight longer than
he fees reafon.* But on either fuppofition, what
evidence is there of a pre-fuppofed Cowardice in *Falftaff*? On the contrary, what
ftronger evidence can we require that
the Courage of *Falftaff* had to this hour,
through various trials, ftood wholly unimpeached, than that *Poins*, the ill-difpofed *Poins*,

K 2   l 4   who

who ventures, for his own purpofes, to fteal, as it
were, *one* of the *four* from the notice and memory of the Prince, and who fhews himfelf,
from worfe motives, as fkilfull in *diminifhing*
as *Falftaff* appears afterwards to be in *increafing*
of numbers, than that this very *Poins* fhould
not venture to put down *Falftaff* in the lift
of Cowards ; though the occafion fo ftrongly
required that he fhould be degraded. What
Poins dares do however in this fort, he *does.*
" *As to the third,*" for fo he defcribes *Falftaff*,
(as if the name of this Veteran would have
excited too ftrongly the ideas of Courage and
refiftance) " *if he fights longer than he fees reafon*
" *I will forfwear arms.*" This is the old trick
of cautious and artful malice : The turn of
expreffion, or the tone of voice does all ;
for as to the words themfelves, fimply confidered, they might be now truly fpoken of
almoft any man who ever lived, except the
iron-headed hero of *Sweden.*—But *Poins* however adds fomething, which may appear more
decifive

decifive; "*The virtue of this jeft will be, the*
"*incomprehenfible lyes which this fat rogue will*
"*tell when we meet at fupper*; *how thirty at*
"*leaft he fought with*; *and what wards, what*
"*blows, what extremities, he endured : And in the*
"*reproof of this lies the jeft* : "—Yes, and the *malice* too.—This prediction was unfortunately
fulfilled, even beyond the letter of it ; a completion more incident, perhaps, to the predic-
tions of malice than of affection. But we
fhall prefently fee how far either the prediction, or the event, will go to the impeachment of *Falftaff*'s Courage.—The Prince, who is
never duped, comprehends the whole of *Poins*'s
views. But let that pafs.

In the next fcene we behold all the parties
at *Gads-Hill* in preparation for the robbery.
Let us carefully examine if it contains any inti-
mation of Cowardice in *Falftaff*. He is fhewn
under a very ridiculous vexation about his
horfe, which is hid from him ; but this is nothing

thing to the purpofe, or only proves that *Fal-ftaff* knew no terror equal to that of walking *eight yards of uneven ground.* But on occafion of *Gadfhill's* being afked concerning the number of the travellers, and having reported that they were eight or ten, *Falftaff* exclaims, " *Zounds !* " *will they not rob us !"* If he had faid more ferioufly, " *I doubt they will be too hard for us,"—* he would then have only ufed the Prince's own words upon a lefs alarming occafion. This cannot need defence. But the Prince, in his ufual ftile of mirth, replies, " *What a* " *Coward, Sir John Paunch !"* To this one would naturally expect from *Falftaff* fome light an-fwer ; but we are furprized with a very feri-ous one ;—" *I am not indeed* John of Gaunt *your* " *grandfather, but yet no* Coward, Hal." This is fingular : It contains, I think, the true cha-racter of *Falftaff* ; and it feems to be thrown out *here,* at a very critical conjuncture, as a caution to the audience not to take too fadly what was intended only (to ufe the Prince's

words)

words,) "*as argument for a week, laughter for* "*a month, and a good jeft for ever after.*" The whole of *Falftaff*'s paft life could not, it fhould feem, furnifh the Prince with a reply, and he is, therefore, obliged to draw upon the coming hope. "*Well*, (fays he, *myfterioufly*,) "*let the event try*;" meaning the event of the concerted attack on *Falftaff*; an event fo probable, that he might indeed venture to rely on it.—But the travellers approach : The Prince haftily propofes a divifion of ftrength ; that he with *Poins* fhould take a ftation feperate from the reft, fo that if the travellers fhould efcape one party, they might light on the other : *Falftaff* does not objeæt, though he fuppofes the travellers to be eight or ten in number. We next fee *Falftaff* attack thefe travellers with alacrity ufing the accuftomed words of threat and terror ;—they make no refiftance, and he binds and robs them.

Hitherto

Hitherto I think there has not appeared the leaft *trait* either of boaft or fear in *Falftaff*. But now comes on the concerted tranf-action, which has been the fource of fo much difhonour. *As they are fharing the booty,* (fays the ftage direction) *the Prince and* Poins *fet upon them, they all run away* ; *and* Falftaff *after a blow or two runs away too, leaving the booty behind them.*—"*Got with much eafe :*" fays the Prince, as an event beyond expectation, "*Now mer-* "*rily to horfe.*"—Poins adds, as they are going off, "*How the rogue roared!*" This obfervation is afterwards remembered by the Prince, who urging the jeft to *Falftaff*, fays, doubtlefs with all the licence of exaggeration,—"*And you* Falftaff, "*carried your guts away as nimbly, with as quick* "*dexterity, and roared for mercy, and ftill ran* "*and roared, as I ever heard bull-calf.*" If he did roar for mercy, it muft have been a very inarticulate fort of roaring ; for there is not a fingle word fet down for *Falftaff* from which this roaring may be inferred, or any ftage direction

rection to the actor for that purpose : But, in the spirit of mirth and derision, the lightest exclamation might be easily converted into the roar of a bull-calf.

We have now gone through this transaction considered simply on its own circumstances, and without reference to any future boast or imputation. It is upon these circumstances the case must be tried, and every colour subsequently thrown on it, either by wit or folly, ought to be discharged. Take it, then, as it stands hitherto, with reference only to its own preceding and concomitant circumstances, and to the unbounded ability of *Shakespeare* to obtain his own ends, and we must, I think, be compelled to confess that this transaction was never intended by *Shakespeare* to detect and expose the false pretences of a real Coward ; but, on the contrary, to involve a man of allowed Courage, though in other respects of a very peculiar character, in such circumstances and

suspicions

fufpicions of Cowardice as might, by the operation of thofe peculiarities, produce afterwards
much temporary mirth among his familiar
and intimate companions : Of this we cannot
require a ftronger proof than the great attention which is paid to the decorum and truth
of character in the ftage direction already
quoted : It appears, from thence, that it was
not thought *decent* that *Falftaff* fhould run at all,
until he had been deferted by his companions,
and had even afterwards exchanged blows
with his affailants ;—and thus, a juft diftinction
is kept up between the natural Cowardice of
the three affociates and the accidental Terror
of *Falftaff*.

Hitherto, then, I think it is very clear
that no laughter either is, or is intended to
be, raifed upon the fcore of *Falftaff*'s Cowardice. For after all, it is not fingularly
ridiculous that an old inactive man of no
boaft, as far as appears, or extraordinary pre-
tenfions

tenſions to valour, ſhould endeavour to ſave himſelf by flight from the aſſault of two bold and vigorous aſſailants. The very Players, who are, I think, the very worſt judges of *Shakeſpeare*, have been made ſenſible, I ſuppoſe from long experience, that there is nothing in this tranſaction to excite any extraordinary laughter; but this they take to be a defect in the management of their author, and therefore I imagine it is, that they hold themſelves obliged to ſupply the vacancy, and fill it up with ſome low buffoonery of their own. Inſtead of the diſpatch neceſſary on this occaſion, they bring *Falſtaff*, *ſtuffing and all*, to the very front of the ſtage; where with much mummery and grimace, he ſeats himſelf down, with a canvaſs money-bag in his hand, to divide the ſpoil. In this ſituation he is attacked by the *Prince* and *Poins*, whoſe tin ſwords hang idly in the air and delay to ſtrike till the *Player Falſtaff*, who ſeems more troubled with flatulence than fear, is able to riſe;

which

which is not till after fome ineffectual efforts,
and with the affiftance, (to the beft of my
memory) of one of the thieves, who lingers
behind, in fpite of terror, for this friendly
purpofe ; after which, without any refiftance on
his part, he is goaded off the ftage like a fat ox
for flaughter by thefe *ftony-hearted* drivers in
buckram. I think he does not *roar* ;—perhaps
the player had never perfected himfelf in
the tones of a bull-calf. This whole tranfaction fhould be fhewn between the interftices
of a back fcene : The lefs we fee in fuch
cafes, the better we conceive. Something of
refiftance and afterwards of celerity in flight
we fhould be made witneffes of ; the *roar* we
fhould take on the credit of *Poins*. Nor is
there any occafion for all that bolftering with
which they fill up the figure of *Falftaff* ; they
do not diftinguifh betwixt humourous exaggeration and neceffary truth. The Prince is
called *ftarveling*, *dried neat's tongue*, *ftock fifh*, and
other names of the fame nature. They might
with

with almoſt as good reaſon, ſearch the glaſs-
houſes for ſome exhauſted ſtoker to furniſh out
a Prince of *Wales* of ſufficient correſpondence
to this picture.

We next come to the ſcene of *Falſtaff*'s braggadocioes. I have already wandered too much into
details ; yet I muſt, however, bring *Falſtaff* forward to this laſt ſcene of trial in all his proper
colouring and proportions. ` The progreſſive
diſcovery of *Falſtaff*'s character is excellently
managed.—In the firſt ſcene we become acquainted with his figure, which we muſt in ſome
degree conſider as a part of his character ; we
hear of his gluttony and his debaucheries, and
become witneſſes of that indiſtinguiſhable mix-
ture of humour and licentiouſneſs which runs
through his whole character ; but what we are
principally ſtruck with, is the eaſe of his
manners and deportment, and the unaffected
freedom and wonderful pregnancy of his wit
and humour. We ſee him, in the next ſcene, agi-

K

tated

tated with vexation: His horfe is concealed from him, and he gives on this occafion fo ftriking a defcription of his diftrefs, and his words fo labour and are fo loaded with heat and vapour, that, but for laughing, we fhould pity him; laugh, however, we muft at the extreme incongruity of a man at once corpulent and old, affociating with youth in an enterprize demanding the utmoft extravagance of fpirit, and all the wildnefs of activity: And this it is which makes his complaints fo truly ridiculous. *" Give me my horfe!"* fays he, in another fpirit than that of *Richard*; *" Eight "yards of uneven ground,"* adds this *Forrefter of Diana,* this *enterprizing gentleman of the fhade,* *" is threefcore and ten miles* a-foot *with me."*— In the heat and agitation of the robbery, out comes more and more extravagant inftances of incongruity. Though he is moft probably older and much fatter than either of the travellers, yet he calls them, *Bacons, Bacon-fed, and gorbellied knaves: " Hang them,* (fays he) *fat chuffs,*
" they

" *they hate us youth: What! young men, muſt*
" *live :—You are grand Jurors, are ye? We'll jure*
" *ye, i' faith.*"   But, as yet, we do not ſee the
whole length and breadth of him : This is reſer-
ved for the braggadocio ſcene.   We expect entertainment, but we don't well know of what kind.
Poins, by his prediction, has given us a hint :
But we do not ſee or feel *Falſtaff* to be a
Coward, much leſs a boaſter ; without which
even Cowardice is not ſufficiently ridiculous ;
and therefore it is, that on the ſtage, we find
them always connected.   In this uncertainty
on our part, he is, with much artful preparation, produced.—His entrance is delayed to
ſtimulate our expectation ; and, at laſt, to take
off the dullneſs of anticipation, and to add ſurprize to pleaſure, he is called in, as if for
another purpoſe of mirth than what we are
furniſhed with : We now behold him, fluc-
tuating with fiction, and labouring with diſ-
ſembled paſſion and chagrin : Too full for
utterance, *Poins* provokes him by a few ſim-

K 2   ple

ple words, containing a fine contraſt of af-
fected eaſe. "*Welcome* Jack, *where haſt thou*
"*been?*" But when we hear him burſt forth,
"*A plague on all Cowards! Give me a cup of ſack.*
"*Is there no virtue extant!*"—We are at once
in poſſeſſion of the whole man, and are ready
to hug him, guts, lyes and all, as an inex-
hauſtible fund of pleaſantry and humour.
Cowardice, I apprehend, is out of our thought ;
it does not, I think, mingle in our mirth.
As to this point, I have preſumed to ſay already, and I repeat it, that we are, in my
opinion, the dupes of our own wiſdom, of
ſyſtematic reaſoning, of ſecond thought, and
after reflection. The firſt ſpectators, I believe,
thought of nothing but the laughable ſcrape
which ſo ſingular a character was falling into,
and were delighted to ſee a humourous and unprincipled wit ſo happily taken in his own
inventions, precluded from all rational defence,
and driven to the neceſſity of crying out, after

ter a few ludicrous evasions, "*No more of that,* "Hal, *if thou lov'ft me.*"

I do not conceive myself obliged to enter into a consideration of *Falftaff*'s lyes concerning the tranfaction at *Gad's-hill.* I have considered his conduct as independent of thofe lyes; I have examined the whole of it apart, and found it free of Cowardice or fear, except in one inftance, which I have endeavoured to account for and excufe. I have therefore a right to infer that thofe lyes are to be derived, not from Cowardice, but from fome other part of his character, which it does not concern me to examine: But I have not contented myfelf hitherto with this fort of negative defence; and the reader I believe is aware that I am refolute (though I confefs not untired) to carry this fat rogue out of the reach of every imputation which affects, or may feem to affect, his natural Courage.

The firft obfervation then which ftrikes us, as to his braggadocioes, is, that they are braggadocioes *after the fact*. In other cafes we fee the Coward of the Play blufter and boaft for a time, talk of diftant wars, and private duels, out of the reach of knowledge and of evidence; of ftorms and ftratagems, and of falling in upon the enemy pell-mell and putting thoufands to the fword; till, at length, on the proof of fome prefent and apparent fact, he is brought to open and *lafting* fhame; to fhame I mean as a *Coward*; for as to what there is of *lyar* in the cafe, it is confidered only as acceffory and fcarcely reckoned into the account of difhonour.—But in the inftance before us, every thing is reverfed: The Play opens with the *Fact*; a Fact, from its circumftances as well as from the age and inactivity of the man, very excufable and capable of much apology, if not of defence. This Fact is preceded by no blufter or pretence whatever;—the lies and braggadocioes follow; but

they

they are not *general*; they are confined, and have reference to this one Fact only; the detection is *immediate*; and after some accompanying mirth and laughter, the shame of that detection ends; it has no *duration*, as in other cases; and, for the rest of the Play, the character stands just where it did before *without any punishment or degradation whatever*.

To account for all this, let us only suppose that *Falstaff* was a man of natural Courage, though in all respects unprincipled; but that he was surprized in one single instance into an act of real terror; which, instead of excusing upon circumstances, he endeavours to cover by lyes and braggadocio; and that these lyes become thereupon the subject, in this place, of detection. Upon these suppositions the whole difficulty will vanish at once, and every thing be natural, common, and plain. The *Fact* itself will be of course *excusable*; that is, it will arise out of a combination of such circumftances, as being applicable to one cafe only, will not deftroy the general character : It will not be *preceded* by any braggadocio, containing any fair indication of Cowardice ; as real Cowardice is not fuppofed to exift in the character. But the firft act of real or apparent Cowardice would naturally throw a vain unprincipled man into the ufe of lyes and braggadocio ; but thefe would have reference only to the *Fact in queftion*, and not apply to other cafes or infect his general character, which is not fuppofed to ftand in need of impofition. Again,—the detection of Cowardice as fuch, is more diverting after a long and various courfe of Pretence, where the lye of character is preferved, as it were, whole, and brought into fufficient magnitude for a burft of difcovery ; yet, mere occafional lyes, fuch as *Falftaff* is hereby fuppofed to utter, are, for the purpofe of fport, beft detected in the telling ; becaufe, indeed, they cannot be preferved for a future time ; the exigence and the

humour

humour will be paſt : But the *ſhame* ariſing to *Falſtaff* from the detection of *mere lyes* would be *temporary only* ; his character as to this point, being already known, and *tolerated for the hu-mour.* Nothing, therefore, could follow but mirth and laughter, and the temporary triumph of baffling a wit at his own weapons, and re-ducing him to an abſolute ſurrender : After which, we ought not to be ſurprized if we ſee him riſe again, like a boy from play, and run another race with as little diſhonour as before.

What then can we ſay, but that it is clearly the lyes only, not the *Cowardice* of *Falſtaff* which are here detected : *Lyes,* to which what there may be of Cowardice is incidental only, improving indeed the Jeſt, but by no means the real Buſineſs of the ſcene.—And now alſo we may more clearly diſcern the true force and meaning of *Poins's* prediction. " *The Jeſt* " *will be,* ſays he, *the incomprehenſible Lyes that*
" *this*

" *this fat rogue will tell us: How thirty at*
" *leaſt he fought with:—and in the reproof of*
" *this lyes the jeſt*;" That is, in the detection
of theſe lyes *ſimply* ; for as to *Courage*, he had
never ventured to inſinuate more than that
Falſtaff would not fight longer than he ſaw
cauſe : *Poins* was in expectation indeed that
Falſtaff would fall into ſome diſhonour on
this occaſion ; an event highly probable : But
this was not, it ſeems, to be the principal
ground of their mirth, but the detection of
thoſe *incomprehenſible lyes*, which he boldly
predicts, upon his knowledge of *Falſtaff*'s character, this *fat rogue*, not *Coward*, would tell
them. This prediction therefore, and the completion of it, go only to the impeachment
of *Falſtaff*'s *veracity* and not of his *Courage*. *Theſe*
" *lyes*, ſays the Prince, *are like the father of*
" *them, groſs as a mountain, open, palpable.—*
" *Why thou clay-brained gutts, thou knotty pa-*
" *ted fool ; how couldſt thou know theſe men in Ken-*
dal

"*dal Green, when it was so dark thou couldst*
"*not see thy hand? Come tell us your reason.*"

"Poins. *Come your reason, Jack, your reason.*"

"Again, says the Prince, *Hear how a plain*
"*Tale shall put you down—What trick, what de-*
"*vice, what starting hole canst thou now find*
"*out to hide thee from this open and apparent*
"*shame?*"

"Poins. *Come let's hear, Jack, what trick*
hast thou now?"

All this clearly refers to *Falstaff*'s lyes only
as such; and the objection seems to be, that
he had not told them well, and with sufficient
skill and probability. Indeed nothing seems to
have been required of *Falstaff* at any period
of time but a good evasion. The truth is,
that there is so much mirth, and so little of
malice or imposition, in his fictions, that they
may

may for the moſt part be conſidered as mere
ſtrains of humour and exerciſes of wit, im-
peachable only for defect, when that happens, of the quality from which they are
principally derived. Upon this occaſion *Falſtaff*'s evaſions fail him ; he is at the end
of his invention ; and it ſeems fair that in
defect of wit, the law ſhould paſs upon him,
and that he ſhould undergo the temporary
cenſure of that Cowardice which he could
not paſs off by any evaſion whatever. The beſt
he could think of, was *inſtinct*: He was indeed a *Coward upon inſtinct*; in that reſpect *like
a valiant lion, who would not touch the true Prince.*
It would have been a vain attempt, the reader will eaſily perceive, in *Falſtaff*, to have
gone upon other ground, and to have aimed
at juſtifying his Courage by a ſerious vindication : This would have been to have miſtaken
the true point of argument: It was his *lyes*,
not his *Courage*, which was really in queſtion.
There was beſides no getting out of the toils

in

in which he had entangled himfelf: If he was not, he ought at leaft, by his own fhewing, to have *been at half-fword with a dozen of them two hours together*; whereas, it unfortunately appears, and that too evidently to be evaded, that he had run with fingular celerity from *two*, after the exchange of *a few blows* only. This precluded *Falftaff* from all rational defence in his own perfon;—but it has not precluded me, who am not the advocate of his *lyes* but of his *Courage*.

But there are other fingularities in *Falftaff*'s lyes, which go more directly to his vindication.—That they are confined to one fcene and one occafion only, we are not *now* at a lofs to account for;—but what fhall we fay to their extravagance? The lyes of *Parolles* and *Bobadill* are brought into fome fhape; but the fictions of *Falftaff* are fo prepofterous and *incomprehenfible*, that one may fairly doubt if they ever were intended for credit; and

therefore

therefore, if they ought to be called *lyes*, and not rather *humour*; or, to compound the matter, *humourous rhodomontades*. Certain it is, that they deftroy their own purpofe and are clearly not the effect, in this refpect, of a regulated practice, and habit of impofition. The real truth feems to be, that had *Falftaff*, loofe and unprincipled as he is, been born a Coward and bred a Soldier, he muft, naturally, have been a great *Braggadocio*, a true *miles gloriofus*: But in fuch cafe he fhould have been exhibited active and young; for it is plain, that age and corpulency are an excufe for Cowardice, which ought not to be afforded him. In the prefent cafe, wherein he was not only involved in fufpicious circumftances, but wherein he feems to have felt fome confcious touch of infirmity, and having no candid conftruction to expect from his laughing companions, he burfts at once, and with all his might, into the moft unweighed and prepofterous fictions, determined to put to proof

on

on this occasion his boasted talent of *swearing truth out of England*. He tried it here, to its utmost extent, and was unfortunately routed on his own ground; which indeed, with such a mine beneath his feet, could not be otherwise. But without this, he had mingled in his deceits so much whimsical humour and fantastic exaggeration that he must have been detected; and herein appears the admirable address of *Shakespeare*, who can shew us *Falstaff* in the various light, not only of what he is, but what he would have been under one single variation of character,—the want of natural Courage; whilst with an art not enough understood, he most effectually preserves the real character of *Falstaff* even in the moment he seems to depart from it, by making his lyes too extravagant for practised imposition; by grounding them more upon humour than deceit; and turning them, as we shall next see, into a fair and honest proof of general Courage, by appropriating them to the conceal-

ment

ment only of a fingle exception. And hence it is, that we fee him draw fo deeply and fo confidently upon his former credit for Courage and atchievment: " *I never dealt better in* " *my life,—thou know'ft my old ward, Hal;*" are expreffions, which clearly refer to fome known feats and defences of his former life. His exclamations againft Cowardice, his reference to his own manhood, " *Die when* " *thou wilt old* Jack, *if manhood, good man-* " *hood, be not forgot upon the face of the earth,* " *then am I a fhotten herring :*" Thefe, and various expreffions fuch as thefe, would be abfurdities not impofitions, Farce not Comedy, if not calculated to conceal fome defect fuppofed unknown to the hearers; and thefe hearers were, in the prefent cafe, his conftant companions, and the daily witneffes of his conduct. If before this period he had been a known and detected Coward, and was confcious that he had no credit to lofe, I fee no reafon why he fhould fly fo violently from a

familiar

familiar ignominy which had often before attached him; or why falfhoods, feemingly in
fuch a cafe, neither calculated for or expecting
credit, fhould be cenfured, or detected, as lyes
or impofition.

That the whole tranfaction was confidered
as a mere jeft, and as carrying with it no ferious imputation on the Courage of *Falftaff* is
manifeft, not only from his being allowed,
when the laugh was paft, to call himfelf,
without contradiction in the perfonated character of *Hal* himfelf, "valiant *Jack Falftaff, and*
" *the more* valiant *being, as he is,* old Jack Falftaff,"
but from various other particulars, and, above
all, from the declaration, which the Prince
makes on that very night of his intention of
procuring this *fat rogue a Charge of foot*;—a
circumftance, doubtlefs, contrived by *Shakefpeare*
to wipe off the feeming difhonour of the day:
And from this time forward, we hear of no
imputation arifing from this tranfaction; it is

L   born

born and dies in a convivial hour; it leaves
no trace behind, nor do we fee any longer
in the character of *Falftaff* the boafting or
braggadocio of a Coward.

Tho' I have confidered *Falftaff*'s character
as relative only to one fingle quality, yet fo
much has been faid, that it cannot efcape the
reader's notice that he is a character made up
by *Shakefpeare* wholly of incongruities ;—a man
at once young and old, enterprizing and fat,
a dupe and a wit, harmlefs and wicked, weak
in principle and refolute by conftitution, cowardly in appearance and brave in reality; a
knave without malice, a lyar without deceit ;
and a knight, a gentleman, and a foldier, without either dignity, decency, or honour : This
is a character, which, though it may be de-
compounded, could not, I believe, have been
formed, nor the ingredients of it duly mingled
upon any receipt whatever : It required the
hand of *Shakefpeare* himfelf to give to every
particular

particular part a relifh of the whole, and of the whole to every particular part ;—alike the fame incongruous, identical *Falftaff*, whether to the grave Chief Juftice he vainly talks of his youth, and offers to *caper for a thoufand*; or cries to Mrs. *Doll*, "*I am old, I am old*," though fhe is feated on his lap, and he is courting her for buffes. How *Shakefpeare* could furnifh out fentiment of fo extraordinary a compofition, and fupply it with fuch appropriated and characteriftic language, humour and wit, I cannot tell; but I may, however, venture to infer, and that confidently, that he who fo well underftood the ufes of incongruity, and that laughter was to be raifed by the oppofition of qualities in the fame man, and not by their agreement or conformity, would never have attempted to raife mirth by fhewing us Cowardice in a Coward unattended by Pretence, and foftened by every excufe of age, corpulence, and infirmity: And of this we cannot have a more ftriking proof than his furnifh-

L 2   ing

ing this very character, on one inftance of real terror, however excufable, with boaft, braggadocio, and pretence, exceeding that of all other ftage Cowards the whole length of his fuperior wit, humour, and invention.

What then upon the whole fhall be faid but that *Shakefpeare* has made certain Impref-fions, or produced certain effects, of which he has thought fit to conceal or obfcure the caufe? How he has done this, and for what fpecial ends, we fhall now prefume to guefs.— Before the period in which *Shakefpeare* wrote, the fools and Zanys of the ftage were drawn out of the coarfeft and cheapeft materials : Some effential folly, with a dafh of knave and coxcomb, did the feat. But *Shakefpeare*, who delighted in difficulties, was refolved to furnifh a richer repaft, and to give to one eminent buffoon the high relifh of wit, humour, birth, dig-nity, and Courage. But this was a procefs which required the niceft hand, and the ut-

moft

moſt management and addreſs : Theſe enumerated qualities are, in their own nature,
productive of *reſpect*; an Impreſſion the moſt
oppoſite to laughter that can be. This Impreſſion then, it was, at all adventures, neceſſary to with-hold; which could not perhaps
well be without dreſſing up theſe qualities in
fantaſtic forms, and colours not their own; and
thereby cheating the eye with ſhews of baſe-
neſs and of folly, whilſt he ſtole as it were
upon the palate a richer and a fuller *goût*.
To this end, what arts, what contrivances, has
he not practiſed ! How has he ſteeped this
ſingular character in bad habits for fifty years
together, and brought him forth ſaturated with
every folly and with every vice not deſtruc-
tive of his eſſential character, or incompatible
with his own primary deſign ! For this end,
he has deprived *Falſtaff* of every good principle; and for another, which will be preſently
mentioned, he has concealed every bad one.
He has given him alſo every infirmity of body

that is not likely to awaken our compaffion, and which is moft proper to render both his better qualities and his vices ridiculous: He has affociated levity and debauch with *age*, corpulence and inactivity with *courage*, and has roguifhly coupled the gout with *Military honours*, and a *penfion* with the *pox*. He has likewife involved this character in fituations, out of which neither wit or Courage can extricate him with honour. The furprize at *Gads-hill* might have betrayed a hero into flight, and the encounter with *Douglas* left him no choice but death or ftratagem. If he plays an after-game, and endeavours to redeem his ill fortune by lies and braggadocio, his ground fails him; no wit, no evafion will avail: Or is he likely to appear refpectable in his perfon, rank, and demeanor, how is that refpect abated or difcharged! *Shakefpeare* has given him a kind of ftate indeed; but of what is it compofed? Of that fuftian cowardly rafcal *Piftol*, and his yoke-fellow of few words the

equally

equally deedlefs *Nym*; of his cup-bearer the fiery *Trigon*, whofe zeal burns in his nofe, *Bardolph*; and of the boy, who bears the purfe with *feven groats and two-pence* ;—a boy who was given him on purpofe to fet him off, and whom he walks *before*, according to his own defcription, " *like a fow that had overwhelmed* " *all her litter but one.*"

But it was not enough to render *Falftaff* ridiculous in his figure, fituations, and equipage; *ftill* his refpectable qualities would have come forth, at leaft occafionally, to fpoil our mirth; or they might have burft the intervention of fuch flight impediments, and have every where fhone through : It was neceffary then to go farther, and throw on him that fubftantial ridicule, which only the incongruities of real vice can furnifh; of vice, which was to be fo mixed and blended with his frame as to give a durable character and colour to the whole.

But it may here be neceſſary to detain the reader a moment in order to apprize him of my further intention; without which, I might hazard that good underſtanding, which I hope has hitherto been preſerved between us.

I have 'till now looked only to the Courage of *Falſtaff*, a quality which having been denied, in terms, to belong to his conſtitution, I have endeavoured to vindicate to the Underſtandings of my readers; the Impreſſion on their Feelings (in which all Dramatic truth conſiſts) being already, as I have ſuppoſed, in favour of the character. In the purſuit of this ſubject I have taken the general Impreſſion of the whole character pretty much, I ſuppoſe, like other men; and, when occaſion has required, have ſo tranſmitted it to the reader; joining in the common Feeling of *Falſtaff*'s pleaſantry, his apparent freedom from ill principle, and his companionable wit and good humour: With a ſtage character, in the arti

cle

cle of exhibition, we have nothing more to
do; for in fact what is it but an Impreffion;
an appearance, which we are to confider as a
reality; and which we may venture to applaud or condemn as fuch, without further inquiry or inveftigation? But if we would account for our Impreffions, or for certain fentiments or actions in a character, not derived
from its apparent principles, yet appearing, we
know not why, natural, we are then compelled
to look farther, and examine if there be not
fomething more in the character than is
fhewn ; fomething inferred, which is not brought
under our fpecial notice : In fhort, we muft
look to the art of the writer, and to the principles of human nature, to difcover the hidden caufes of fuch effects.—Now this is a
very different matter—The former confiderations refpected the Impreffion only, without
regard to the Underftanding; but this queftion
relates to the Underftanding alone. It is true
that there are but few Dramatic characters
which

which will bear this kind of inveſtigation, as
not being drawn in exact conformity to thoſe
principles of general nature to which we muſt
refer. But this is not the caſe with regard to
the characters of *Shakeſpeare*; they are ſtruck
out *whole*, by ſome happy art which I cannot
clearly comprehend, out of the general maſs of
things, from the block as it were of nature:
And it is, I think, an eaſier thing to give a
juſt draught of man from theſe Theatric forms,
which I cannot help conſidering as originals,
than by drawing from real life, amidſt ſo
much intricacy, obliquity, and diſguiſe. If
therefore, for further proofs of *Falſtaff*'s Courage, or for the ſake of curious ſpeculation,
or for both, I change my poſition, and look
to cauſes inſtead of effects, the reader muſt
not be ſurprized if he finds the former *Falſtaff*
vaniſh like a dream, and another, of more diſ-
guſtful form, preſented to his view; one, whoſe
final puniſhment we ſhall be ſo far from re-
gretting, that we ourſelves ſhall be ready to
conſign him to a ſeverer doom.

The

The reader will very eafily apprehend that
a character, which we might wholly difap-
prove of, confidered as exifting in human life,
may yet be thrown on the ftage into certain
peculiar fituations, and be compreffed by external influences into fuch temporary appearances, as may render fuch character for a time
highly acceptable and entertaining, and even
more diftinguifhed for qualities, which on this
fuppofition would be accidents only, than another character really poffeffing thofe qualities,
but which, under the preffure of the fame fituation and influences, would be diftorted into
a different form, or totally loft in timidity and
weaknefs.   If therefore the character before
us will admit of this kind of inveftigation,
our Inquiry will not be without fome dignity,
confidered as extending to the principles of
human nature, and to the genius and arts of
Him, who has beft caught every various form of
the human mind, and tranfmitted them with the
greateft happinefs and fidelity.

To

To return then to the vices of *Falstaff.*—
We have frequently referred to them under
the name of ill habits;—but perhaps the reader is not fully aware how very vicious he indeed is;—he is a robber, a glutton, a cheat,
a drunkard, and a lyar; lascivious, vain, info-
lent, profligate, and profane:—A fine infusion
this, and such as without very excellent cook-
ery muft have thrown into the dish a great
deal too much of the *fumet.* It was a nice operation;—thefe vices were not only to be of a
particular fort, but it was alfo neceffary to
guard them at both ends; on the *one,* from
all appearance of malicious motive, and indeed
from the manifeftation of any ill principle
whatever, which muft have produced *difguft,*—
a fenfation no lefs oppofite to laughter than is
refpeɛt;—and, on the *other,* from the notice, or
even apprehenfion, in the fpeɛtators, of *pernicious
effeɛt*; which produces *grief* and *terror,* and is
the proper province of Tragedy alone.

Actions cannot with strict propriety be said
to be either virtuous or vicious. These qualities, or attributes, belong to *agents* only; and
are derived, even in respect to *them*, from intention alone. The abstracting of qualities,
and considering them as independent of any
subject, and the applying of them afterwards
to actions independent of the agent, is a double operation which I do not pretend, thro'
any part of it, to understand. All actions
may most properly, in their own nature, I
think, be called *neutral*; tho' in common dif-
course, and in writing where precision is not
requisite, we often term them *vicious*, transferring on these occasions the attributive from
the *agent* to the *action*; and sometimes we call
them *evil*, or of pernicious effect, by transferring, in like manner, the injuries incidentally arising from certain actions to the life,
happiness, or interest of human beings, to the
natural operation, whether moral or physical,
of the *actions* themselves: *One* is a colour
thrown

thrown on them by the *intention*, in which I
think confifts all moral turpitude, and the
other by effect: If therefore a Dramatic
writer will ufe certain managements to keep
vicious intention as much as poffible from
our notice, and make us fenfible that no
evil effect follows, he may pafs off actions
of very vicious motive, without much ill impreffion, as mere *incongruities*, and the effect
of *humour* only;—*words thefe*, which, as applied to human conduct, are employed, I believe, to cover a great deal of what may deferve much harder appellation.

The *difference* between fuffering an evil effect to take place, and of preventing fuch
effect, from actions precifely of the fame nature, is fo great, that it is often *all the difference* between Tragedy and Comedy. The Fine
gentleman of the Comic fcene, who fo
promptly draws his fword, and wounds, without killing, fome other gentleman of the
fame

fame fort; and *He* of Tragedy, whofe ftabs
are mortal, differ very frequently in no other
point whatever. If our *Falftaff* had really
peppered (as he calls it) *two rogues in buckram
fuits*, we muft have looked for a very different
conclufion, and have expected to have found
Falftaff's Effential profe converted into blank
verfe, and to have feen him move off, in
flow and meafured paces, like the City Pren-
tice to the tolling of a Paffing bell;—" *he*
" *would have become a cart as well as another,*
" *or a plague on his bringing up.*"

Every incongruity in a rational being is a
fource of laughter, whether it refpects manners, fentiments, conduct, or even drefs, or fituation;—but the greateft of all poffible incongruity is vice, whether in the intention itfelf, or as transferred to, and becoming more
manifeft in action;—it is inconfiftent with moral
agency, nay, with rationality itfelf, and all the
ends and purpofes of our being.—Our author
defcribes

defcribes the natural ridicule of vice in his
MEASURE *for* MEASURE in the ftrongeft
terms, where, after having made the angels
weep over the vices of men, he adds, that
with our fpleens *they might laugh themfelves quite
mortal.* Indeed if we had a perfect difcernment
of the ends of this life only, and could
preferve ourfelves from fympathy, difguft and
terror, the vices of mankind would be a
fource of perpetual entertainment. The great
difference between *Heraclitus* and *Democritus* lay,
it feems, in their fpleen only;—for a wife and
good man muft either laugh or cry without
ceafing. Nor indeed is it eafy to conceive
(to inftance in one cafe only) a more
laughable, or a more melancholy object, than
a human being, his nature and duration confidered, earneftly and anxioufly exchanging
peace of mind and confcious integrity for
gold; and for gold too, which he has often
no occafion for, or dares not employ :—But
                                              Voltaire

Voltaire has by one Publication rendered all *arguments* fuperfluous : He has told us, in his *Candide*, the merrieft and moft diverting tale of frauds, murders, maffacres, rapes, rapine, defolation, and deftruction, that I think it poffible on any other plan to invent ; and he has given us *motive* and *effect*, with every poffible aggravation, to improve the fport. One would think it difficult to preferve the point of ridicule, in fuch a cafe, unabated by contrary emotions ; but now that the feat is performed it appears of eafy imitation, and I am amazed that our race of imitators have made no efforts in this fort : It would anfwer I fhould think in the way of profit, not to mention the moral ufes to which it might be applied. The managements of *Voltaire* confift in this, that he affumes a gay, eafy, and light tone himfelf ; that he never excites the reflections of his readers by making any of his own ; that he hurries us on with fuch a rapidity of narration as prevents our

M

emotions

emotions from resting on any particular point; and to gain this end, he has interwoven the conclusion of one fact so into the commencement of another, that we find ourselves engaged in new matter before we are sensible that we had finished the old; he has likewise made his crimes so enormous, that we do not sadden on any sympathy, or find ourselves partakers in the guilt.—But what is truly singular as to this book, is, that it does not appear to have been written for any moral purpose, but for That only (if I do not err) of satyrising Providence itself; a design so enormously profane, that it may well pass for the most ridiculous part of the whole composition.

But if vice, divested of disgust and terror, is thus in its own nature ridiculous, we ought not to be surprised if the very same vices which spread horror and desolation thro' the Tragic scene should yet furnish the Comic

with

with its higheſt laughter and delight, and that
tears, and mirth, and even humour and wit
itſelf, ſhould grow from the ſame root of
incongruity : For what is humour in the hu-
mouriſt, but incongruity, whether of ſentiment,
conduct, or manners ? What in the man of
humour, but a quick diſcernment, and keen
ſenſibility of theſe incongruities ? And what is
wit itſelf, without preſuming however to give
a complete definition where ſo many have
failed, but a talent, for the moſt part, of
marking with force and vivacity unexpected
points of likeneſs in things ſuppoſed incongruous, and points of incongruity in things ſuppoſed alike : And hence it is that wit and humour,
tho' always diſtinguiſhed, are ſo often coupled
together ; it being very poſſible, I ſuppoſe, to
be a man of humour without wit ; but I
think not a man of wit without humour.

But I have here raiſed ſo much new matter,
that the reader may be out of hope of ſee-

ing

ing this argument, any more than the tale of *Triftram*, brought to a conclufion : He may fuppofe me now prepared to turn my pen to a moral, or to a dramatic Effay, or ready to draw the line between vice and virtue, or Comedy and Tragedy, as fancy fhall lead the way;—But he is happily miftaken; I am prefing earneftly, and not without fome impatience, to a conclufion. The principles I have now opened are neceffary to be confidered for the purpofe of eftimating the character of *Falftaff*, confidered as relatively to human nature : I fhall then reduce him with all poffible difpatch to his Theatric condition, and reftore him, I hope, without injury, to the ftage.

There is indeed a vein or two of argument running through the matter that now furrounds me, which I might open for my own more peculiar purpofes ; but which, having refifted much greater temptations, I fhall wholly defert. It ought not, however, to be forgotten,

that

that if *Shakefpeare* has ufed arts to abate our
refpect of *Falftaff*, it fhould follow by juft
inference, that, without fuch arts, his character would have grown into a *refpect* inconfiftent with laughter ; and that yet, without
Courage, he could not have been refpectable
at all ;—that it required nothing lefs than the
union of ability and Courage to fupport his
other more accidental qualities with any tole-
rable coherence. Courage and Ability are firft
principles of Character, and not to be deftroyed
whilft the united frame of body and mind continues whole and unimpaired ; they are the
pillars on which he ftands firm in fpight of
all his vices and difgraces ;—but if we fhould
take Courage away, and reckon Cowardice a-
mong his other defects, all the intelligence
and wit in the world could not fupport him
through a fingle Play.

The effect of taking away the influence
of this quality upon the manners of a cha-

racter, tho' the quality and the influence be aſſumed only, is evident in the caſes of *Parolles*
and *Bobadil*. *Parolles*, at leaſt, did not ſeem
to want wit ; but both theſe characters are reduced almoſt to non-entity, and after their
diſgraces, walk only thro' a ſcene or two, the
mere mockery of their former exiſtence. *Parolles*
was ſo changed, that neither the *fool*, nor the
old lord *Le-feu*, could readily recollect his
perſon ; and his wit ſeemed to be annihilated
with his Courage.

Let it not be here objected that *Falſtaff* is
univerſally conſidered as a Coward ;—we do
indeed call him ſo ; but that is nothing,
if the character itſelf does not act from any
conſciouſneſs of this kind, and if our Feelings take his part, and revolt againſt our
underſtanding.

As to the arts by which *Shakeſpeare* has
contrived to obſcure the vices of *Falſtaff*, they
are

are fuch, as being fubfervient only to the mirth of the Play, I do not feel myfelf obliged to detail.

But it may be well worth our curiofity to inquire into the compofition of *Falftaff*'s character.—Every man we may obferve, has two characters; that is, every man may be feen externally, and from without;—or a fection may be made of him, and he may be illuminated from within.

Of the external character of *Falftaff*, we can fcarcely be faid to have any fteady view. *Jack Falftaff* we are familiar with, but *Sir John* was better known, it feems, *to the reft of Europe*, than to his intimate companions; yet we have fo many glimpfes of him, and he is opened to us occafionally in fuch various points of view, that we cannot be miftaken in defcribing him as a man of birth and fafhion, bred up in all the learning and accomplifhments of

N 2   the

the times ;—of ability and Courage equal to any fituation, and capable by nature of the higheft affairs; trained to arms, and poffeffing the tone, the deportment, and the manners of a gentleman ;—but yet thefe accomplifhments and advantages feem to hang loofe on him, and to be worn with a flovenly careleffnefs and in-attention : A too great indulgence of the quali-ties of humour and wit feems to draw him too much one way, and to deftroy the grace and orderly arrangement of his other accom-plifhments;—and hence he becomes ftrongly marked for one advantage, to the injury, and almoft forgetfulnefs in the beholder, of all the reft. Some of his vices likewife ftrike through, and ftain his Exterior;—his modes of fpeech betray a certain licentioufnefs of mind; and that high Ariftocratic tone which belong-ed to his fituation was pufhed on, and aggravated into unfeeling infolence and oppref-fion. " *It is not a confirmed brow*," fays the Chief

Juftice,

Juſtice, "*nor the throng of words that come with*
"*ſuch more than impudent ſaucineſs from you, can*
"*thruſt me from a level conſideration :*" " *My lord,*
anſwers *Falſtaff,* "*you call honourable boldneſs im-*
"*pudent ſaucineſs. If a man will courtſie and ſay*
"*nothing, he is virtuous : No my lord, my humble*
"*duty remembered, I will not be your ſuitor. I ſay*
"*to you I deſire deliverance from theſe officers, being*
"*upon haſty employment in the King's affairs.*"
"*You ſpeak,* replies the Chief Juſtice, "*as hav-*
"*ing power to do wrong.*"—His whole behaviour
to the Chief Juſtice, whom he deſpairs of
winning by flattery, is ſingularly inſolent; and
the reader will remember many inſtances of
his inſolence to others : Nor are his manners
always free from the taint of vulgar ſociety;
—"*This is the right fencing grace, my lord,*" (ſays he
to the Chief Juſtice, with great impropriety of
manners) "*tap for tap, and ſo part fair :*" " *Now*
"*the lord lighten thee,*" is the reflection of the
Chief Juſtice, "*thou art a very great fool.*"—

Such

Such a character as I have here described,
strengthened with that vigour, force, and alacrity
of mind, of which he is possessed, must have
spread terror and dismay thro' the ignorant,
the timid, the modest, and the weak : Yet is
he however, when occasion requires, capable of
much accomodation and flattery;—and in order
to obtain the protection and patronage of the
great, so convenient to his vices and his poverty, he was put under the daily necessity of
practising and improving these arts ; a base-
ness, which he compensates to himself, like
other unprincipled men, by an increase of insolence towards his inferiors.—There is also
a natural activity about *Falstaff*, which for
want of proper employment, shews itself in a
kind of swell or bustle, which seems to cor-
respond with his bulk, as if his mind had
inflated his body, and demanded a habitation
of no less circumference : Thus conditioned
he rolls (in the language of *Ossian*) like a *Whale
of Ocean*, scattering the smaller fry; but afford-
ing

ing, in his turn, noble contention to *Hal* and *Poins*; who, to keep up the allufion, I may be allowed on this occafion to compare to the Threfher and the Sword-fifh.

To this part of *Falftaff*'s character, many things which he does and fays, and which appear unaccountably natural, are to be referred.

We are next to fee him *from within* : And here we fhall behold him moft villainoufly unprincipled and debauched; poffeffing indeed the fame Courage and ability, yet ftained with numerous vices, unfuited not only to his primary qualities, but to his age, corpulency, rank, and profeffion ;—reduced by thefe vices to a ftate of dependence, yet refolutely bent to indulge them at any price. Thefe vices have been already enumerated; they are many, and become ftill more intolerable by an ex-

cefs

cefs of unfeeling infolence on one hand, and of bafe accomodation on the other.

But what then, after all, is become of *old Jack?* Is this the jovial delightful companion—*Falflaff*, the favourite and the boaft of the Stage?—by no means. But it is, I think however, the *Falflaff* of Nature; the very ftuff out of which the *Stage Falflaff* is compofed; nor was it poffible, I believe, out of any other materials he could have been formed. From this difagreable draught we fhall be able, I truft, by a proper difpofition of light and fhade, and from the influence and compreffion of external things, to produce *plump Jack*, the life of humour, the fpirit of pleafantry, and the foul of mirth.

To this end, *Falflaff* muft no longer be confidered as a fingle independent character, but grouped, as we find him fhewn to us in the Play;—his ability muft be difgraced by buffoonery,

buffoonery, and his Courage by circumftances of
imputation; and thofe qualities be thereupon
reduced into fubjects of mirth and laughter :—
His vices muft be concealed at each end from
vicious defign and evil effect, and muft thereupon be turned into incongruities, and affume
the name of humour only;—his infolence muft
be repreffed by the fuperior tone of *Hal* and
Poins, and take the fofter name of fpirit only,
or alacrity of mind;—his ftate of dependence, his temper of accomodation, and his activity, muft fall in precifely with the indulgence of his humours; that is, he muft thrive
beft and flatter moft, by being extravagantly
incongruous ; and his own tendency, impelled
by fo much activity, will carry him with
perfect eafe and freedom to all the neceffary
exceffes. But why, it may be afked, fhould
incongruities recommend *Falftaff* to the favour
of the Prince ?—Becaufe the Prince is fuppofed to poffefs a high relifh of humour
and

and to have a temper and a force about him, which, whatever was his purfuit, delighted in excefs. This, *Falftaff* is fuppofed perfectly to comprehend; and thereupon not only to indulge himfelf in all kinds of incongruity, but to lend out his own fuperior wit and humour againft himfelf, and to heighten the ridicule by all the tricks and arts of buffoonery for which his corpulence, his age, and fituation, furnifh fuch excellent materials. This compleats the Dramatic character of *Falftaff*, and gives him that appearance of perfect good-nature, pleafantry, mellownefs, and hilarity of mind, for which we admire and almoft love him, tho' we feel certain referves which forbid our going that length; the true reafon of which is, that there will be always found a difference between mere appearances, and reality: Nor are we, nor can we be, infenfible that whenever the action of external influence upon him is in whole or in part relaxed, the character reftores

itfelf

itſelf proportionably to its more unpleaſing condition.

A character really poſſeſſing the qualities which are on the ſtage imputed to *Falſtaff*, would be beſt ſhewn by its own natural ener-gy; the leaſt compreſſion would diſorder it, and make us feel for it all the pain of ſym-pathy: It is the artificial condition of *Falſtaff* which is the ſource of our delight; we enjoy his diſtreſſes, we *gird at him* ourſelves, and urge the ſport without the leaſt alloy of compaſſion; and we give him, when the laugh is over, undeſerved credit for the pleaſure we enjoyed. If any one thinks that theſe obſervations are the effect of too much refinement, and that there was in truth more of chance in the caſe than of management or deſign, let him try his own luck;—perhaps he may draw out of the wheel of fortune a *Macbeth*, an *Othello*, a *Benedict*, or a *Falſtaff*.

Such

Such, I think, is the true character of this extraordinary buffoon; and from hence we may difcern for what fpecial purpofes *Shakefpeare* has given him talents and qualities, which were to be afterwards obfcured, and perverted to ends oppofite to their nature; it was clearly to furnifh out a Stage buffoon of a peculiar fort; a kind of Game-bull which would ftand the baiting thro' a hundred Plays, and produce equal fport, whether he is pinned down occafionally by *Hal* or *Poins*, or toffes fuch mongrils as *Bardolph*, or. the Juftices, fprawling in the air. There is in truth no fuch thing as totally demolifhing *Falftaff*; he has fo much of the invulnerable in his frame that no ridicule can deftroy him; he is fafe even in defeat, and feems to rife, like another *Antæus*, with recruited vigour from every fall; in this as in every other refpect, unlike *Parolles* or *Bobadil*: They fall by the firft fhaft of ridicule, but *Falftaff* is a butt on which we may empty the whole quiver, whilft the

fubftance

fubftance of his character remains unimpaired.
His ill habits, and the accidents of age and
corpulence, are no part of his effential conftitution ; they come forward indeed on our
eye, and folicit our notice, but they are
fecond natures, not *firft*; mere fhadows, we
purfue them in vain ; *Falftaff* himfelf has
a diftinct and feparate fubfiftence ; he laughs
at the chace, and when the fport is over,
gathers them with unruffled feather under his
wing : And hence it is that he is made to
undergo not one detection only, but a feries
of detections; that he is not formed for one
Play only, but was intended originally at
leaft for two; and the author we are told, was
doubtful if he fhould not extend him yet
farther, and engage him in the wars with
France. This he might well have done, for
there is nothing perifhable in the nature of
Falftaff: He might have involved him, by the
vicious part of his character, in new difficulties and unlucky fituations, and have enabled

N

him

him, by the better part, to have fcrambled through, abiding and retorting the jefts and laughter of every beholder.

But whatever we may be told concerning the intention of *Shakefpeare* to extend this character farther, there is a manifeft preparation near the end of the fecond part of Henry IV. for his difgrace : The difguife is taken off, and he begins openly to pander to the exceffes of the Prince, intitling himfelf to the character afterwards given him of being *the tutor and the feeder of his riots.* " *I will fetch* " *off,*" (fays he) " *thefe Juftices.—I will devife* " *matter enough out of this* Shallow *to keep the Prince* " *in continual laughter the wearing out of fix* " *fafhions.—If the young* dace *be a bait for the* " *old* pike," (fpeaking with reference to his own defigns upon *Shallow*) " *I fee no reafon in* " *the law of nature but I may fnap at him.*"— This is fhewing himfelf abominably diffolute: The laborious arts of fraud, which he prac-

tices

tices on *Shallow* to induce the loan of a thoufand pound, create *difguft*; and the more,
as we are fenfible this money was never likely
to be *paid back*, as we are told that *was*, of
which the travellers had been robbed. It is
true we feel no pain for *Shallow*, he being a
very bad character, as would fully appear,
if he were unfolded; but *Falftaff*'s deliberation
in fraud is not on that account more excufable.—The event of the old King's death
draws him out almoft into deteftation.--" *Maf-*
"*ter* Robert Shallow, *chufe what office thou wilt*
" *in the land,*—'*tis thine.*—*I am fortune's fteward.*—
" *Let us take any man's horfes.*—*The laws of Eng-*
" *land are at my commandment.*—*Happy are they*
" *who have been my friends;*—*and woe to my*
" Lord Chief Juftice."—After this we ought not
to complain if we fee Poetic juftice duly ex-
ecuted upon him, and that he is finally given
up to fhame and difhonour.

But

But it is remarkable that, during this procefs, we are not acquainted with the fuccefs
of *Falftaff*'s defigns upon *Shallow* 'till the moment of his difgrace. "*If I had had time,*" (fays
he to *Shallow,* as the King is approaching,)
"*to have made new liveries, I would have beftowed*
"*the thoufand pounds I borrowed of you;*"—and
the firft word he utters after this period is,
"*Mafter* Shallow, *I owe you a thoufand pounds :*"
We may from hence very reafonably prefume, that *Shakefpeare* meant to conneᵈt this
fraud with the punifhment of *Falftaff,* as a
more avowed ground of cenfure and difhonour : Nor ought the confideration that this
paffage contains the moft exquifite comic humour and propriety in another view, to diminifh the truth of this obfervation.

But however juft it might be to demolifh
Falftaff in this way, by opening to us his
bad principles it was by no means *convenient.*
If we had been to have feen a fingle reprefentation

fentation of him only, it might have been
proper enough; but as he was to be fhewn
from night to night, and from age to age, the
difguft arifing from the *clofe*, would by degrees have fpread itfelf over the whole character; reference would be had throughout to
his bad principles, and he would have become lefs acceptable as he was more known:
And yet it was neceffary to bring him, like
all other ftage characters, to fome conclufion.
Every play muft be wound up by fome event,
which may fhut in the characters and the action.
If fome *hero* obtains a crown, or a miftrefs,
involving therein the fortune of others, we
are fatisfied;—we do not defire to be afterwards admitted of his council, or his bed-
chamber: Or if through jealoufy, caufelefs
or well founded, *another* kills a beloved wife,
and himfelf after,—there is no more to be
faid;—they are dead, and there an end;
Or if in the fcenes of Comedy, parties are
engaged, and plots formed, for the furthering

or

or preventing the completion of that great
article Cuckoldom, we expect to be fatisfied
in the point as far as the nature of fo nice
a cafe will permit, or at leaft to fee fuch a
manifeft *difpofition* as will leave us in no
doubt of the event. By the bye, I cannot but
think that the Comic writers of the laft age
treated this matter as of more importance,
and made more buftle about it, than the
temper of the prefent times will well bear;
and it is therefore to be hoped that the
Dramatic authors of the prefent day, fome
of whom, to the beft of my judgment, are de-
ferving of great praife, will confider and treat
this bufinefs, rather as a common and natural incident arifing out of modern manners,
than as worthy to be held forth as the
great object and fole end of the Play.

But whatever be the queftion, or whatever
the character, the curtain muft not only be dropt
before

before the eyes, but over the minds of the ſpectators, and nothing left for further examination and curioſity.—But how was this to be
done in regard to *Falſtaff*? He was not involved in the fortune of the Play; he was engaged in no action which, as to him, was to
be compleated; he had reference to no ſyſtem,
he was attracted to no center; he paſſes thro'
the Play as a lawleſs meteor, and we wiſh to
know what courſe he is afterwards likely to
take: He is detected and diſgraced, it is
true; but he lives by detection, and thrives
on diſgrace; and we are deſirous to ſee him
detected and diſgraced again. The *Fleet* might
be no bad ſcene of further amuſement;—he
carries *all* within him, *and what matter* where,
if he be ſtill the ſame, poſſeſſing the ſame force
of mind, the ſame wit, and the ſame incongruity. This, *Shakeſpeare* was fully ſenſible of,
and knew that this character could not be
compleatly diſmiſſed but by death.—" Our
" author, (ſays the Epilogue to the Second
" Part

" Part of Henry IV.) will continue the ſtory
" with Sir *John* in it, and make you merry
" with fair *Catherine* of *France* ; where, for any
" thing I know, *Falſtaff* ſhall dye of a ſweat,
" unleſs already he be killed with your hard
" opinions." If it had been prudent in
Shakeſpeare to have killed *Falſtaff* with *hard opi-*
nion, he had the means in his hand to effect
it ;—but dye, it ſeems, he muſt, in one form
or another, and a *ſweat* would have been no un-
ſuitable cataſtrophe. However we have reaſon
to be ſatisfied as it is ;—his death was worthy
of his birth and of his life : " *He was born,*
he ſays, " *about three o'clock in the afternoon with*
a white head, and ſomething a round belly."
But if he came into the world in the even-
ing with theſe marks of age, he departs
out of it in the morning in all the follies
and vanities of youth ;—" *He was ſhaked* (we
" are told) " *of a burning quotidian tertian;—*
" *the young King had run bad humours on the*
" *knight;—his heart was fracted and corroborate;*
" *and*

"*and a' parted juft between twelve and one, even*
"*at the turning of the tide, yielding the crow a*
"*pudding, and paffing directly into* Arthur's bofom,
"*if ever man went into the bofom of* Arthur."—
So ended this fingular buffoon; and with him
ends an Effay, on which the reader is left
to beftow what character he pleafes: An Effay
profeffing to treat of the Courage of *Falftaff*,
but extending itfelf to his Whole character;
to the arts and genius of his Poetic-Maker,
SHAKESPEARE; and thro' him fometimes, with
ambitious aim, even to the principles of human nature itfelf.

THE END.

E R R A T A.[1]

Page. line
49, 8, (in the notes) for *Henry* VI. read *Henry* IV.
50, 3, (in the notes) correct the same error
60, the last but two in the notes, for be *this* when thou art dead—read—be *thus*, &c.
65, 13, for the plains of *Sciola*—read—the plains of *Sciota*.
78, 9, for *as* far—read—*so* far.
84, 14, for *minching malicho*—read—*miching malicho*.
105, 6 and 7, for goes off the sickly effort—read—goes off *in* the sickly effort.
108, the last but one, for *bare*—read—*base*.
109, 18, for *circumstances*—read—*circumstance*.

In a few of the copies

172, 4, for *the jovial delightful companion*—read—*Is this the jovial*, &c.

[1] [*Corrected in this reprint.*]

THE OXFORD MISCELLANY

¶ Poetry : Reproductions of Original Editions

BROWNING. Men and Women, 1855. The two volumes in one.

BURNS. The Kilmarnock Edition, 1786. Reprinted in type-facsimile

COLERIDGE & WORDSWORTH. Lyrical Ballads, 1798 Edited by H LITTLEDALE.

COLLINS. Poems. With facsimile title-pages, three illustrations, and a Memoir by CHRISTOPHER STONE.

GRAY. Poems, 1768. Reprinted in type-facsimile, with four illustrations

KEATS. Lamia, Isabella, The Eve of St. Agnes, and other Poems, 1820. A page for-page and line-for-line reprint, with a facsimile title-page.

SHELLEY (MARY). Proserpine and Midas. Two unpublished Mythological Dramas Edited by A. KOSZUL

SHELLEY. Prometheus Unbound, with other Poems, 1820

TENNYSON. Poems, 1842.

WORDSWORTH. Poems, 1807.

¶ Selections from the Poets

BARNES (WILLIAM). Edited with a Preface and glossarial notes by THOMAS HARDY.

BLAKE. The Lyrical Poems. With an Introduction (45 pages) by Sir WALTER RALEIGH, and two drawings by Blake

CLARE (JOHN). Introduction by ARTHUR SYMONS.

CLOUGH. The Bothie, and other Poems. Edited by H S MILFORD.

DE TABLEY (LORD). With an Introduction by JOHN DRINKWATER

PRAED (WILLIAM MACKWORTH). Edited by A D GODLEY With a portrait.

THE OXFORD MISCELLANY

¶ Fiction

BARRETT (E. S.). *The Heroine, or Adventures of a fair Romance Reader (1813)*. With an Introduction by Sir WALTER RALEIGH.

GALT (JOHN). *Annals of the Parish (1821)*. With an Introduction by G S GORDON, and a frontispiece and facsimile title-page.

INCHBALD (MRS.). *A Simple Story (1791)*. With an Introduction by LYTTON STRACHEY, and facsimile title-page.

PEACOCK (T. L.). *Nightmare Abbey*. A page-for-page reprint of the first edition, 1818. Edited by C E. JONES.

READE (CHARLES). *A Good Fight (1859)*. The original short version of *The Cloister and the Hearth*. Here for the first time reprinted in book-form. With an Introduction by ANDREW LANG, and fourteen illustrations by CHARLES KEENE.

WOLLSTONECRAFT (MARY). *Original Stories* from Real Life. Introduction by E V. LUCAS, with five illustrations by W. BLAKE.

¶ Anthologies

ECHOES FROM THE OXFORD MAGAZINE, 1883–1890.

MORE ECHOES FROM THE OXFORD MAGAZINE, 1890–1896. With contributions by Sir ARTHUR QUILLER-COUCH and his contemporaries

SEA-SONGS AND BALLADS, 1400–1886. With an Introduction by Admiral Sir CYPRIAN BRIDGE.

TREASURY OF SACRED SONG, from Dunbar to Tennyson. Selected by FRANCIS TURNER PALGRAVE. Also on Oxford India paper, 4s 6d net.

WAR-SONGS, 1333–1866. Selected by CHRISTOPHER STONE. With an Introduction by General Sir IAN HAMILTON.

WORDSWORTH. *Poems and Extracts chosen by Wordsworth* (from the Countess of Winchelsea and others) for an album, Christmas, 1819, and now first printed Introduction by H. LITTLEDALE and Preface by J. R. REES. With a portrait and facsimile

THE OXFORD MISCELLANY

¶ Travel and Topography

CURZON (ROBERT). Visits to Monasteries in the Levant. With an Introduction by D G HOGARTH. Illustrated.

KINGLAKE (A. W.). Eothen. With an Introduction by D. G. HOGARTH, and two illustrations.

LOWELL (JAMES RUSSELL). Fireside Travels. With an Introduction by E. V LUCAS.

MORITZ (CARL PHILIPP). Travels in England in 1782. With an Introduction by P. E. MATHESON, and three illustrations

WORDSWORTH (WILLIAM). A Guide to the Lakes. With an Introduction by E DE SÉLINCOURT, and eight contemporary illustrations.

DUFF-GORDON (LADY). Letters from the Cape. Edited by JOHN PURVES.

¶ Literary History and Criticism

COLERIDGE. Literary Criticism. Introduction by J W. MACKAIL

DE QUINCEY. Literary Criticism. Introduction by HELEN DARBISHIRE

HURD. Letters on Chivalry and Romance. Introduction by EDITH MORLEY.

JEFFREY. Literary Criticism. Introduction by D. NICHOL SMITH.

JOHNSON ON SHAKESPEARE. Essays and Notes selected and set forth with an Introduction by Sir WALTER RALEIGH.

JOHNSON. Selections from 'The Rambler'. Introduction by W. HALE WHITE, with a portrait and two other illustrations

MORGANN. Essay on Sir John Falstaff, 1777. A page-for-page and line-for-line reprint Introduction by W. A. GILL.

THE OXFORD ARS POETICA. Edited by W. E. BROWNING, with an Introduction by G. S. GORDON. [*In the Press.*

PEACOCK (T. L). Memoirs of Shelley. With Shelley's Letters to Peacock, and two portraits. With an Introduction by H F. B. BRETT SMITH

SHELLEY. Literary and Philosophical Criticism. With an Introduction by JOHN SHAWCROSS.

3

THE OXFORD MISCELLANY

SHELLEY. Prose in the Bodleian Manuscripts. Edited by A. H. KOSZUL.

TRELAWNY. Recollections of the Last Days of Shelley and Byron. With two portraits and two other illustrations. Introduction by E. DOWDEN.

WORDSWORTH. Literary Criticism. Introduction by NOWELL C. SMITH.

WORDSWORTH. Tract on the Convention of Cintra, 1809. Introduction by A. V. DICEY.

¶ Miscellaneous

COBBETT. Grammar of the English Language. Introduction by Sir H. L. STEPHEN.

COBBETT. Advice to Young Men, and (incidentally) to Young Women, 1829. With a facsimile title-page.

THE HAMBLEDON MEN. John Nyren's Young Cricketer's Tutor. Edited with other matter from various sources by E. V. LUCAS. With twenty-two illustrations, and a ' Ballade of Dead Cricketers ' by ANDREW LANG.

JOWETT. Theological Essays. With an Introduction by LEWIS CAMPBELL.

JOWETT. Scripture and Truth. Introduction by LEWIS CAMPBELL.

¶ Three Japanese Classics
Translated by W. N. PORTER

A HUNDRED VERSES FROM OLD JAPAN. With 100 reproductions of Japanese woodcuts.

THE TOSA DIARY. Written in A.D. 935. Translation, with notes and a map of the voyage from Tosa to Kyōto.

THE MISCELLANY OF A JAPANESE PRIEST, being the Tsure-zure Gusa, 1337-9. With seven reproductions of Japanese woodcuts, and an Introduction by SANKI ICHIKAWA.

OXFORD UNIVERSITY PRESS
Humphrey Milford, Amen House, London, E.C. 4

January, 1925

This book is DUE on the last date stamped below

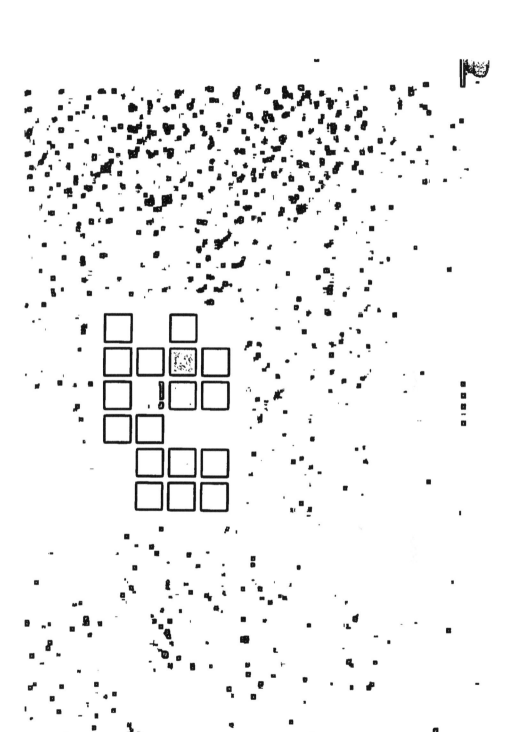